Things I
Learned
from
Falling

Things I Learned from Falling

Claire Nelson

aster

To all those who are lost,
and to the ones who go out searching.

And for Mum and Dad.
You were resilient first.

An Hachette UK Company
www.hachette.co.uk
First published in Great Britain in 2020 by Aster, an imprint of
Octopus Publishing Group Ltd
Carmelite House
50 Victoria Embankment
London EC4Y 0DZ
www.octopusbooks.co.uk

Text and illustrations copyright © Claire Nelson 2020

Distributed in the US by Hachette Book Group
1290 Avenue of the Americas
4th and 5th Floors
New York, NY 10104
Distributed in Canada by Canadian Manda Group
664 Annette St.
Toronto, Ontario, Canada M6S 2C8

ISBN 978-1-78325-350-0

A CIP catalogue record for this book is available from the British Library.
Printed and bound in the UK

10 9 8 7 6 5 4 3 2 1

Some names have been changed to protect people's identity.

Publishing director: Stephanie Jackson
Senior editor: Pauline Bache
Copyeditor: Liz Marvin
Art director: Juliette Norsworthy
Cover Designer: Luke Bird
Designer: Jeremy Tilston at The Oak Studio
Production Manager: Lisa Pinnell

Contents

Prelude

I remember the sound my body made as it hit the ground.

A sharp crack. One that cut through the thump of my weight against the desert floor. Then the white heat of pain that stabbed through my body, escaping through my mouth in an almighty howl.

I tried to scramble to my feet – the instinctive reaction to falling – but I couldn't get up. Everything below the arms remained a dead weight.

Get up.

I heaved my head and shoulders forward, trying to prise myself off the ground, but each time I crumpled. Again. And again. And again. Something in my body was disconnected. Urgent messages were being fired from the brain but they weren't getting through.

Only pain. Unbearable, indescribable pain, a scorching flame-gun that set me alight with each attempt to move.

Sprawled, flat on my back, my breathing was fast and loud. I craned my neck to get a look at my legs. I couldn't lift them either. Or bend my knees.

Oh god.

Oh god, please no...

My feet were also immovable, weighted to the desert floor, but I found with intense concentration I could lean them slightly from side to side.

I gently wiggled my toes inside my boots.

OK. I wasn't paralysed. That was something. I felt a strange flicker of hope through the pain and panic, a sense of, 'I'm going to be alright.'

But my pelvis was broken. That much was clear. *Shattered* was actually the word that kept coming to my mind: more than a break, it felt like there were *pieces*. Every time I tried to sit up, it felt like someone had replaced my hip bones with a bag of broken dinner plates, shards jangling loosely, so my shoulders could do nothing but slump back to the ground.

As the realization of the extent of my injuries set in so did the cold tingle of shock, and my teeth began to chatter uncontrollably, like wind-up dentures, a violently loud clacking inside my head.

Help.

My daypack had dislodged from my shoulder when I'd fallen but was thankfully within reach. I yanked it towards me, scrabbling in the front pocket for my iPhone, my hands shaking as I dialled 911. All the while my brain raced to scramble a request together.

An ambulance, right? I needed an ambulance. Of some sort. Some medical aid. Any medical aid. I just needed help.

Out of the corner of my eye, on the screen pressed to my ear, I saw words flash up: Call Failed.

No. No no no.

I dialled again: Call Failed.

I checked the phone and saw I had zero bars. A horrifying and crushing realization hit me with the full force of its weight:

I am out of phone range here.

My stomach lurched; of course I am out of range, I am in the middle of the California desert. It's why I'd had my phone tucked away in the rucksack – I wouldn't need it here. Except now I did need it, and I had no other means of communication.

You fucking idiot, roared the voice in my head, now dark and furious. How had I been so stupid? No, no, this had to work. This couldn't be happening. Clinging desperately to denial, I held the phone high up in every direction I could, whispering silent pleas for a miracle as my heart banged loudly in my chest, my eyes locked on the corner of the iPhone screen where the little bars would normally be.

I was miles from a signal. Miles from the road. Miles into the middle of nowhere.

I knew I was out of luck. I knew.

Yet I couldn't stop trying. And with each redial, each attempt to reach out to someone, anyone, any other human being on this planet, just to let someone know I was here and I was hurt, the absolute futility of it sunk in deeper. With each press of the button my hope melted into cold fear.

Call Failed.

Redial.

Call Failed.

Redial.

Call Failed.

Redial.

Call Failed.

I screamed into the sky as loudly as I could – HELP ME! PLEASE! And I heard the echoes dissolve into the rocks around me, absorbed like rain drops, until all that was left was silence.

Day One:
Tuesday

I was halfway across Joshua Tree National Park when I saw the coyote. A movement had caught my eye as the car idled on the side of the road, a glimpse of something large through the driver's window. I felt that gently prickling sensation you get when someone's gaze is on you. Turning my head, there it was, standing some ten feet away among the scrub and cacti, watching me with eyes as grey as its scruffy, dusty coat. I stared back.

Hi.

The usual instinct took over, making me reach for my camera, my hand slowly moving to where I'd nestled it in the well of the car door. Just then the coyote moved too – trotting quickly away, shaggy tail hanging low, tongue lolling. It crossed in front of the car, paws dancing across the tar seal, and once on the sand of other side of the road it stopped again, turned its head and looked back at me.

What are you thinking, coyote?

If you could talk, what would you tell me?

I had just crossed the high desert portion of Joshua Tree National Park, following the turns of the road through the swathes of spiny Joshua trees that seemed to stretch for miles on either side, singing along to my favourite driving playlist. I sang loudly, liberated by the fact there was nobody even remotely nearby to hear me. I felt so utterly free out here. I had space to breathe; precisely the thing I had left my life in England to try to pin down. I thought of the stress I'd felt in packing up my flat and leaving London. How overloaded I had felt, how burned out and broken. And I had done it – I'd left it all behind. Said farewell to London and all of the accoutrements of the life I had built there, on the road to find whatever it was I was missing. Heading for the great outdoors.

Sometime during my recent travels I'd read an article about the experiences of astronauts who, after bearing witness to planet earth from space, described an overwhelming awareness and profound sense of universal connectedness; something that came to be known as 'the overview effect'. An emotional response sparked by a greater perspective. And I'd realized that within the course of my own life trajectory I'd lost my overview. Maybe I was just too busy looking inward.

What I was missing was a sense of awe. What I needed was to feel not just inspired and connected but inspired by and connected to something that was real and solid and which asked nothing more of me than to be myself.

Perhaps this is what led me to seek solitude in the outdoors, in the great wide open. And now I was here. Revelling in it. It was hard not to feel very satisfied when I thought of all the decisions made to get me to this point – driving through the desert, with no one around for miles.

Fleetwood Mac's 'Rhiannon' came up on the playlist. I was immediately taken back to the first time I'd come here, to Joshua Tree. A side trip after a friend's wedding. There had been five of us then, packed into a boxy rental, elbows slung out of windows, the hits of Fleetwood Mac playing on repeat – one of the only albums anyone had available offline on their phone. I remember being so mesmerized by this place; the strangeness of the trees slipping past, the landscape as alien as anything I'd ever seen. I remember the details of that day so vividly: watching the road ahead through the frame of the front seats. The slosh of the water keg in the back. My hand hanging out the rear passenger window, pressing against the hot metal of the car door until my fingertips felt the burn, then stretching out into nothing, my fingers pushing through the thick, warm desert air.

'It's as if Dr Seuss had sketched the backdrop for a Western,' I'd scrawled in my notebook later. 'You'd think there's little life in these places, but there is plenty, and it has a greater capacity for survival in this extreme climate than you or I.' That first dalliance had stayed with me, never forgotten, tucked away in my pocket of golden memories like a holiday romance.

It felt good to be back. This time, though, I had it all to myself.

The road dipped as the park shifted towards the low desert, the southern side of the national park. This was the Colorado desert, strikingly different from that of the high Mojave I'd left behind, a whole other ecosystem. Here it was drier, hotter and more barren, and the tufty-fingered Joshua trees had gone, replaced by sprawling gardens of squat, spiny cholla cactus and tall, spindly ocotillos. It opened up before me, the most magnificent vista of the low valley, rocky canyons lit up in melting gold by the rising morning sun.

Wow.

Pulling the car to the side of the road, I sat there for a minute or two, just looking at it. Taking it in. If I didn't have some place to be, I could easily have sat there for a long while, watching the light change, the shape of the landscape shifting with it.

And that was when I saw the coyote, watching me. As I pulled the car back on to the road, it trotted alongside – for a moment, at least, accompanying me.

What are you thinking, coyote?

Is there something you wanted to tell me?

By the time I looked back in the rear-view mirror, it was gone.

———————

I wasn't even meant to go to California. After I packed up my life in the UK, and cleared out all my belongings, I had stepped on board a plane to Canada. The plan, if you could call it that, was to spend a few months on the road, travelling from province to province, exploring places I'd never been, and immersing myself in the great outdoors. I had visions of standing among lakes and mountains and snow-topped pines, and maybe being out there amongst it all I would find a way to yank myself out of the rut I was stuck in. I was going to start again, some place else. Some place new. My visa offered me two years, so these initial travels would also serve as reconnaissance, helping me to decide where I might want to drop anchor. I was already thinking Vancouver: I'd never been but, nestled between mountains, ocean and forest, it seemed to offer everything I needed. What I was seeking was change. Life in London had left me burned out and bruised. I felt hollow, anxious, lost. It felt like my identity and self-worth were no longer linked to anything rooted, only in the fleeting and the temporary, things that would be gone again in a moment. Like a social-media post. Or my freelance work as a writer – features pitched, laboured over, published, only to become next month's recycling.

My day job as a magazine sub-editor was constant high pressure and frenzied push-and-pull over the most minute detail. Then, the second everything was sent to the printer, without any fanfare, we'd immediately crack on with the next issue's content. By the time the printed magazine hit my desk I couldn't even look at it. My head saturated, it had moved on to the next thing. And I moved on, like I was always moving on, never feeling like my feet were firmly on the ground. I'd adapted to the environment I was living in – short term. The painful irony was that I'd spent a long time building a short-term life, 13 years maintaining a house of straw. It felt so hard to hold on to anything any more. Even people came and went all the time; my social circle, scattered wildly around the globe, had become a testament to that.

The very place that had drawn me in with its alluring perpetual motion had left me running on empty. It wasn't London's fault, it was mine – be careful for what you wish for, isn't that how the saying goes? I was born a moving cog and had attached myself to a spinning machine...when what I really needed, deep down, was something strong and stable to place my footing on.

It was the tail-end of winter when I flew from Heathrow to Toronto, landing on the snow-scuffed doorstep of my good friend Caroline, one of my London friends since moved on, returned to her home province. I'd missed her. There were few people in my life I felt I could let my mask down with and she was one. Just her presence made me realize how much I wanted to be free of it entirely.

Of course, I was here to make things happen, chase the change I needed. That first week or so I'd spent the days walking around Toronto, basking in the warmth of different coffee shops, hunched over my laptop and studiously pitching feature ideas to travel magazines. I wanted to believe I had left behind the nagging fear of pitching my ideas and the voice of self-doubt. Change location, change habits.

I will make this happen.

To my surprise, things quickly started paying off. My very first pitch was accepted and I was sent to Montreal to write about maple syrup. From there, I picked my way around Quebec's rugged expanse and the eastern edges of Ontario, making everything up as I went along, being open to opportunities and enjoying the freedom of not knowing what would come next. I would see where the Canadian wind blew me.

I just hadn't expected it to blow me into California.

The invitation had come from Natalie and Lou – former London friends from way back – who were now living in Joshua Tree, California. Did I want to come to the desert and house-sit for three weeks?

Yes, yes, yes!

I had gone looking for wilderness and now it had found me.

I'd always found something appealing about a desert – a place that seems barren on the surface but will reveal its secrets to those who take the time to stop and pay attention. My fascination with such places was first sparked on a trip to Morocco some eight years before. I had arranged a week in the Sahara with my then-boyfriend Ben, a young camel-hand, a guide, and three laden camels. It had seemed the grandest adventure of my life, a chance to channel my inner wannabe explorer. Of course, I wasn't an explorer, I was an editorial assistant living in a shared ex-council flat in Southwark. But still – I could pretend. I could be a dollar-store Thesiger for a brief moment.

And in the end, I got my wish. A true adventure. On our second morning, all three of the camels escaped their tethers and disappeared, dissolving into the horizon. We were stranded. Ben and I kept watch over the supplies – warding off groups of hungry ranging goats – while our guides set off on foot to try to track down the fugitive animals, without success. That evening we built a fire, luring our guides back to us in the dark, and our little crew improvised a new plan over pots of sugary mint tea, broken English and French and campfire songs played on an out-of-tune guitar. Any itinerary had blown away on the sands and suddenly I was having the time of my life. I felt so happy, then. I remember sitting atop a plateau as the sun began to sink into the horizon, seeing the miles and miles of uninterrupted nothingness, feeling an incredible ease.

'We are so far from anywhere recognizable,' I wrote in my notebook. 'The shapes in the sand are beautiful and everywhere we look there are tracks of different kinds, each with its own pattern of repetition. I love being here. Sitting on this hill in the Sahara I feel really alive.'

It was a feeling I had again in the desert of southern California – an altogether different creature, more rock than sand, where the life that teems within it is found a little closer to the surface. But still a glorious wealth of emptiness. In Joshua Tree National Park alone there's a whopping 800,000 acres of nothingness – an area more than twice the size of Greater London but consisting of nothing but miles of rolling, hilly desert and rocky canyons, peppered with giant boulders and the eponymous trees with their strange, tufty fingers.

The desert is beautiful, peaceful, uncluttered – a world regenerating daily with the slow, steady rhythm of the earth. Everything that London is not.

I'd arrived at the house late, in pitch dark. Natalie and husband Lou were away on the first part of their travels. They'd be back for a brief stopover before venturing off again to Morocco for business, then to Scotland, for a wedding. But for now, I would get my bearings. And I would begin my adventure with a small sunrise hike. It was not quite dawn as I heaved myself out of bed, feeling a sense of excitement – surprisingly alert for 5am – and padded down the hall to the kitchen in search of coffee.

I'd first met Natalie, a plucky Australian, in my early twenties, a few months after arriving in London. I'd applied to be her new housemate, made the cut, and we had lived in a pokey flat in an ex-council building in Bayswater, west London. It was one of those brutalist estates built back in the 1950s, once a grand example of modernist inner-city living, now characterized by looming concrete, square patches of grass and elevators with an acrid, metallic smell that stung the nose. The walls of the bathroom would crumble grit into the tub whenever anyone had a shower and the only communal hang-out space was the tiny kitchen.

Being the hapless romantic I am, I found this all terribly charming. Natalie and I were both working as temps – her as a legal secretary, me as a travel consultant – and, given that work was intermittent, we were living on a shoestring much of the time. But we tried our best to make it feel like a home. Our landlord, in a rare moment of leniency, had let us redecorate – albeit on the proviso we keep all walls the same bland shade of magnolia. Instead, we bought cheap pots of paint from a hardware shop in Ladbroke Grove and painted garishly bright feature walls; I transformed a whole wall of my bedroom in a vibrant shade of turquoise, a colour that cheered me. For however long I would occupy this space, I would make it my own. I still think of that time fondly as the broccoli and gravy era, on account of our dinners of frozen veggies doused in Bisto, saving money for more important things, like red wine. Always the optimist, I had a habit of romanticizing everything about the world I inhabited. We might be broke but we were living in this film-set of a city with its rich layers of history.

Since we were not far from Notting Hill, my favourite way to while away a Saturday was to wander down through the pillared cafés and boutiques of Westbourne Grove and pick myself up a slice of cake from the Hummingbird Bakery. I'd take my time strolling the entire length of Portobello Road market, eating my cake out of the box with a wooden fork and absorbing myself in the eclectic mix of vintage and vagrant, watching merchants polishing antique silverware while next door reggae blared from a boombox, admiring the trinkets and treasures with the awe of Alice as she wandered through Wonderland. I was smitten.

London was all I'd hoped for. A place where, even if my dreams were not made real, there was at least the delicious possibility that they could be. A city so connected with the rest of the world, in the thick of it all, where stories had been written, told, and played out for centuries upon centuries. And now, mine would be one of them. My London life could be a romance novel, a travel epic and a Choose Your Own Adventure book in one. This was the place where I could redesign the course of my life, shaping everything I'd dreamed of into something tangible, and real and mine.

It wasn't long after I moved in that Natalie met Lou and his friends, affable Americans from the Midwest, fellow expats, all of us enjoying a camaraderie built upon our shared appreciation for what felt new and novel in an exciting, aged city (basically, just about everything). Before long, Lou and Natalie packed up and left the crumbling council flat and the two of them became citizens of the world, at one time or another living in his hometown of Chicago, or her hometown of Sydney. A life on the move, constantly soothing their perpetually itchy feet. I would meet up with them from time to time, in different places, different chapters, tied by this sense of longing to find a place to belong to.

Now they were creating one. Setting up a life in Joshua Tree, putting their heart and soul into building a property. Their home in the meantime was a single-level ranch house, sitting high on a half-acre of dusty desert overlooking the distant expanse of the pale, terracotta peaks and troughs that marked the outskirts of the National Park. Not that I could see any of that yet – it was early and still dark. Nothing to note but a big sky full of stars.

I found the coffee, made a pot, then set about feeding their two affectionate cats, creatures as well travelled as their owners, and currently circling my ankles. Given my friends were renting this place, they were limited to what they could do with it, but I could see Nat had already put her stamp on it, trying her best to make it feel like theirs, decorating it with thick-pile rugs and cacti and wicker shelving. There were boards of images, her design plans for their building project. I felt a swell of pride for my old friend and what she was making for herself. We had long since grown out of our slap-dash feature walls.

We had long since grown up.

Through the kitchen window I could see the first signs of dawn on the very distant horizon, a hint of a watercolour pink, bringing the edge of the faraway hills into layered silhouette. I breathed in deeply and let out a sigh. I felt happy here. In a way that I hadn't for quite some time.

———————

Natalie was explaining the risks of getting lost in unmarked desert. After a couple of days on my own she and Lou were back for a brief stopover between trips – a chance to catch up and for them to show me around.

'It's very easy to lose your way,' she'd warned me. 'It happens out here all the time.'

The three of us were picking our way through Section 6, an undeveloped conservation area along the Onaga Trail, popular with walkers and dirt bikes. Here, among a square mile of rough dunes and rocky ridges, there were vague suggestions of trails but no marked path. I could only rely upon my friends' familiarity with the landscape and our collective sense of direction as we hiked in a loop, the idea being that we would eventually find our way back to the car.

We ambled on through Section 6, the terrain rising and rolling away all around us. Lou was leading the route and prodding the ground with his hiking stick. I'd picked up a long, skinny tree branch and was absentmindedly poking the ground with it as I walked, looking out for snakes. I sort of hoped I might see one.

'You want to borrow the stick for a bit?' offered Lou, waving it towards me.

He was so proud of that thing: an acquisition from a recent trip, bought from a guy in Arkansas who carves them by hand. It was roughly three feet long, made of dark wood with an ellipses-shaped knob on the top. Rustic, but it suited the terrain.

'Thanks, I'm good though.'

'It's an awesome stick...' he said, his voice going up at the end as it does when he's trying to sell a point. I laughed.

'Yep, it's awesome...But no. Thanks, though.'

I didn't tend to walk with a stick. Occasionally when I was tackling hills, like on hikes in the rugged Welsh ranges, or on the steep climbs of England's Lake District. Most of the time, though, carrying a stick only seemed cumbersome. I was already growing tired of wielding my tree branch, and I let it drop to the sand.

'All riiiight,' said Lou, giving up on his pitch for the moment. 'But you should take it walking when we're away.'

I grinned. 'Maybe.'

The three of us were geared up in boots, neck-bandanas and hats, yet despite it being only mid-morning the heat of the day was already threatening to bake through the swiftly fading layers of sunscreen that lingered on our skin. In every direction the scenery was a repetitive backdrop of rolling sandy dunes, dotted with rocks and many varieties of squat, virulent cacti – a landscape that seemed to repeat itself over and over, all the while constantly changing. It was like David Bowie's labyrinth out here. I could see how it would be very easy to get lost.

And by the sounds of it, it really did happen often. As we strode on through the rocky dunes, they told me some tales of tragedies that had befallen people in this desert, locals and visitors alike. Recent scenarios included an elderly man who, despite years of living in the area, found himself in trouble, collapsing from exhaustion before being found three days later on the brink of death. A retired couple suffered overheating and dehydration. They had to be airlifted out, but sadly the wife did not make it. A young couple reported missing in the park, search parties slowly scaling back as the weeks went on, and three months later the last determined searchers discovering their bodies somewhere deep in the park. Searchers had found the pair locked in an embrace. It had become local lore, but it was heartbreaking. People trying to survive in such a difficult place.

These stories sent a shiver up my spine. I couldn't imagine going through such a thing. It's a hard and hostile environment out there in the desert. Soaring temperatures, unyielding terrain, no obvious landmarks to find your way back.

I told myself I'd stick to established trails.

I knew my friends were right to warn me about the risks of being out here on my own and I nodded gravely, taking in their stories. But, somehow, I didn't think they applied to me. I had it in my head that I knew what I was doing. I could take care of myself. I figured it was one thing to follow my friends through this patch of open desert, but when on my own I would only tackle the marked trails, and they would be a piece of cake. There was no tingle of risk, no red flag, no concern about my plans to hike on my own. After all, out here I felt more comfortable and in my element than I had back in the city.

I had my heart set on completing as many trails as I could. Proximity to the outdoors was something I had been missing in my life and here I was with this national park and its surrounding desert right on my doorstep! I decided that I'd start small, to give myself a chance to get used to the terrain, and by week two I'd reward myself with something longer, something I could get my teeth into.

And there was one in particular that I had in mind.

Lou and Natalie had told me about the Lost Palms Oasis, an in-and-out hike of a little over four miles each way, leading to a large congregation of palms hidden deep in a valley. As soon as I heard about it I was dead certain I'd walk it. It was, like so many of the trails in the park, one that any visitor could just rock up and do. The only reason I gave it any special regard was that it was long enough to require planning for: a hike of about four hours. Plus, it was on the south side of Joshua Tree National Park – meaning it would take an hour and a half to drive each way across the park to get to the trailhead. These were factors that excited me. A dream solo day out: a long, scenic drive followed by a long, scenic hike. I was itching to go.

Lou had left me the keys to his beloved Mini Cooper – a manual, or stick-shift, as I'd quickly learned to call it. He'd had that thing for longer than I'd known him. It hardly seemed the most ideal car for the desert but he wouldn't drive anything else and had brought it all the way down from Chicago. I still remembered visiting him and Natalie there, not long after they'd moved away from London, for a Fourth of July weekend in the Windy City. How Lou had driven that Mini with five of us tightly crammed in, and severely hungover, to a Six Flags theme park for the day.

'This might be the worst idea anyone ever had,' I'd groaned from the back seat, suffering through my self-inflicted nausea.

That day felt like for ever ago. Yet here it was, the same car, in California, still going strong. Just like we all were.

'Be super careful with it,' he'd said.

'Ah, man, there go my plans for some off-roading,' I'd teased. But I knew I'd be lucky if I took it as high as the speed limit. That he trusted me with it had touched me more than I could let on, so I was especially determined he would come back to find the car without a scratch on it.

I couldn't have known the car would fare better than I would.

I dropped the two of them at the airport in Palm Springs for the first flight of the day, driving back gingerly through the dark desert roads as the sun began to climb over the landscape, bringing the Joshua trees into silhouette. I stalled at the lights once or twice as I got used to driving a stick-shift, but my confidence grew with every mile. Like so many other new dalliances outside my comfort zone, I would get the hang of this too. I now had two weeks left out here, which on one hand seemed a lot, but I knew it would fly by, and I was hungry to devour as much of the desert as I could.

The next week of my residence was, in my books at least, productively spent, getting in daily hikes coupled with scenic drives along the area's endless straight roads. I made a handwritten calendar, a table scrawled crudely on a sheet of lined paper. Squares and dates, ready for me to lay out trails. A map, as it were, of my hiking plans.

I began by visiting some of the gentler spots outside of the confines of the national park, the very first being a sunrise walk to the Fortynine Palms Oasis, the sandy path undulating and zig-zagging its way around large, dusky boulders, the landscape turning to colour in the light of the morning sun. The sudden reveal at the end was a fistful of palm trees sunken in the valley, their tropical lushness seeming so out of place in the dry and scrubby setting. The trunks of the palms were cocooned in the old, dead branches they had shed for newer, greener foliage over the innumerable years they had stood here. I clambered up a large boulder beside them and stood still, letting total silence surround me.

I'm not a religious person. I don't believe in a god, not in the classic sense of deities and judgement. The great outdoors...that is the altar I worship at. This is where I pray. Nature does not judge. It asks for nothing but respect.

Every trail in the area offered something unique, and every day another opportunity. One afternoon I ventured up South Park Peak, a straightforward amble on the edge of the Little San Bernardino Mountains, the dusty trail lined with juniper and lichen, climbing up, up, up, until finally I was rewarded with unobstructed views from Black Rock Canyon and across the vast, flat plains of Yucca Valley, stretching out to the distant mountains.

Another day, I took the little unmarked trail down to Coyote Hole, accessible from the house; a path through land once used by Native Americans – possibly the Serrano and Chemehuevi – as evident from the petroglyphs tattooed into the rocks high above the ground. Natalie had shown me the path on a stroll one evening, but now, trying to find it on my own, I lost sight of it. The route we had followed from behind the street looked different now, even though it was only days later, and once I reached the point where the trail intersected the tar-sealed road I no longer remembered which way to continue. As I scanned the land beyond the road my instincts seemed to point in one direction, but moving closer I saw nothing familiar and my confidence was dwindling by the minute. Not far from where I stood, on the side of the road, a large, scabby vulture was hunched over the remains of what had been either a chipmunk or a ground squirrel, black feathers twitching with each tear of flesh. I thought about the stories my friends had told me of locals getting lost even close to home and noted the shadows of early evening were already beginning to stretch long across the landscape. Best not to risk it.

I glanced behind me, the street still in view, the tips of houses peeking over the top of the dunes. The vulture lifted its head from the bloody mound of fur and fixed its beady eyes on me with something I could only presume was curiosity.

'Dream on, mate,' I said, and turned back for the house.

I'd decided to keep all the hikes I wanted to do in Joshua Tree National Park for week two. A park pass cost $25 and lasted seven days, so it made sense to do the park trails in one hit, and by then I'd also be more used to the desert terrain.

I got out my hiking calendar. There was one walk I was particularly excited about, so I decided to do it first. A Tuesday would be best, I thought. Nice and quiet. Not too busy. And with a committed nod, I wrote on the hand-drawn scrawl of my calendar, underneath 22 May, the words:

Lost Palms Oasis.

The night before I set off on my day hike, I gathered anything I thought I might need, preparing everything so I could set off good and early.

I wouldn't need much. It was a day trip. Just a few bits and pieces.

I planned to wear my usual get-up of old denim shorts, a cotton vest and my beloved hiking boots, which I'd bought in Toronto my first week in Canada. They were from the men's department, as so many of my shoes and hats tended to be, blessed as I am with a big head and big feet. The man in the store told me the manufacturers had originally made aircraft tyres in the 1920s, until the Second World War, at which point they turned their rubber facilities to making boots for French legionnaires. I couldn't help being romanced by the idea of wearing boots with a genealogy in aviation pioneers and elite battle forces, but it wasn't the story that suckered me in. They were simply the most comfortable boots I'd ever worn. When I put them on it felt like I was supposed to be wearing them all along. I felt they could take me anywhere I wanted to go.

Southern California in late May gets pretty hot, too hot to need a jacket. But as someone who had spent more than a decade living in England, I felt a discomforting nakedness in not taking *some* sort of extra layer. And it would be wise to have some extra coverage from the sun should I start to burn.

Slip, Slop, Slap.

I could still hear the 1980s TV jingle of childhood; a goofy cartoon seagull citing the importance of being sun smart.

Slip on a T-shirt, slop on some sunscreen and slap on a hat!

Suffice to say, it was deeply embedded in me to have all three covered.

I set aside my straw hat, as well as my favourite T-shirt – the one I'd got at a Bob Dylan concert last year, when I was still in London, and emblazoned with the lyrics *Listen to that Duquesne Whistle Blowing*. It was a size too big on account of me buying it after two plastic cups of Wembley Arena-grade whisky. But the fact it was a little oversized meant it would make a great throw-on layer.

As for the sunscreen, that was already in the crude first-aid kit I'd thrown together: various accoutrements from my toiletry bag that might be handy. Into a clear Ziploc sandwich bag I'd tossed a couple of Band-Aids (in case of blisters), tweezers (in case of cacti spines), toilet paper and hand sanitizer (because you never know what the facilities offer), a bit of physio tape that I habitually carried around in case my old wrist injury flared up and – largely because I'd slept badly and woken up with a stiff, sore neck – some Tylenol. I'd popped a couple with breakfast and as there were only a few left rattling around in the small jar, I lazily threw the whole thing in.

Lunch was a bagel, sliced and slathered with avocado, a hard-boiled egg and a chocolate-chip Cliff bar. That would be more than enough to see me through till dinner. I found I didn't have the biggest appetite in this heat, and I had it in my head that if, after the hike, I found myself too ravenous to wait until I got home, I could stop for a bite in Yucca Valley. Hell, if I finished early enough, perhaps I'd even take the longer route back, go through Palm Springs, and take my pick from the strip of drive-through fast-food joints. I'd only been driving a few months so the concept of a picking up a drive-through meal was a novelty. So, I had options, but no plan. That was all part of the fun.

I'd see where the wind blew me.

I made sure I packed my digital camera. Even now, in the age of smartphones, I hadn't entirely shaken the habit of having a camera with me. When I first moved to London I was renowned for always having one to hand, always taking photos. There was no Instagram yet, no Facebook, so the photos were almost entirely for my own benefit. Although it meant I was one hundred per cent that annoying friend who was always whipping out a camera. It didn't matter what my friends and I were doing – late-night rickshaw races through the frenetic streets of Chinatown, or drinking in our favourite shabby wine bar – I'd be trying to catch it all in a freeze-frame.

'She's got that damned camera again,' Tessa – one of the American friends I'd met through Lou – would protest, partly in jest and partly because I was being a total pain in the arse. Always snapping away. My friends called me 'Paparazzi', but in time both the photo-taking and the protesting of it became woven into the fabric of our friendships. Any annoyance would give way to expectation the next day when everyone wanted to see the pictures I'd captured. The evidence – for better or for worse – of our good times.

That's what it always was for me. Wanting to capture it, preserve even the smallest, most stupid moments, so I could hold on to them for ever. So that they never had to end. Because in the back of my mind I knew that eventually, everything ends.

Finally – water. I took as much as I could comfortably carry: two one-litre bottles and a three-litre CamelBak water bladder, all filled, chilled and ready to go. Enough water to last the day.

In a rare fit of packing minimalism I'd left my pack behind in Caroline's garage in Toronto with my winter clothing and the detritus of my travelling gear. So I sent Lou a text:

```
Hey, do you have a little day pack I could
borrow? Gonna do Lost Palms Oasis tomorrow…
```

Lou replied with instructions on where to find a small blue rucksack. Early the next morning I packed up my gear and slung it on the passenger seat of the car with my hat. I was ready to roll. But as I began to reverse out of the driveway I had a sudden nagging feeling, a strange sensation that I couldn't quite place.

Wait.

I'll never know what compelled me to go back into the house. But the feeling was significant enough to make me stop the car. I switched off the ignition, hurried back up the path, unlocked the front door and reached just inside, grabbing Lou's wooden hiking stick from where it leaned against the wall in the hallway.

I was running late. I had planned to be on the trail by 8.30am at the latest, setting off early with the intention to beat the heat, but it was almost 9am when I pulled into the Cottonwood Visitors Centre. Being late stresses me out. But not only was I running behind schedule, I was a bit lost. The trailhead was proving tricky to find. The offline map I'd downloaded to my iPhone brought me somewhere in the vicinity – my little blue GPS dot hovering near the red pin icon that marked the trailhead car park – but never quite meeting it. I watched the dot get closer and closer and then...I'd passed it again.

Well, I should probably stop in at the visitor's centre anyway.

Once inside the small shady building, I let my eyes adjust and looked around at the usual tourist accessories. Stacks of guidebooks and Californian travel literature. Postcards with stock images of Joshua Trees and colourful illustrations of UFOs. Refrigerators chilling bottles of water and cans of soda. Boxes of protein snack bars and chocolate. I approached the desk and returned the smile of the ranger manning it.

'Morning!' I said brightly, then pulled a sheepish grin. 'I'm a bit lost, I think...I'm trying to find the Lost Palms Oasis trail.'

'Ah! You're very close,' he replied, and raised his arm to point to a turn-off just behind the centre which would, he assured me, lead to the Cottonwood Trailhead. This whole time I was only a few minutes away.

'So, hiking to the oasis, huh?' he asked, which I suppose was a rhetorical question, but I nodded anyway, and took the opportunity to ask about the route: what's the trail like? Is there anything I should be aware of?

In truth, I was not only checking for guidance on the route... I was also thinking about bees.

That summer I'd come to Joshua Tree with friends, it had been mid-July, creeping close to the peak of the season's scorching heart, and swarms of bees had been a problem in the park. At certain viewing spots signs announced 'Beware of the Bees', and indeed, when returning from the top of Keys View lookout to the car park, we found our vehicle surrounded by a fuzzy cloud of them. The swarm was sniffing out water, closing in on anything that might offer sustenance. Eventually, one of the guys made a stealth dash to the driver's door, leaped in and started driving away to shake off the bees, as the rest of us ran after it, leaping in and slamming the doors of the moving vehicle – 'Go, go go!' – like we'd just robbed a bank.

Today, according to the ranger, the main concern was the heat.

'The temperature out there is pretty serious this time of the year,' he explained. 'So just make sure you have a lot of water with you.'

'I've got five litres. I should be OK, right?'

He nodded. 'Great! Sounds just right.'

He handed me a neatly folded map of the park and I took it, although I already had one in my rucksack.

'I should mention there is a bit of a scramble once you get to the valley...so as long as you're comfortable with climbing over rocks.'

I nodded.

'It's not actually that bad,' he assured me. 'Just that most of the effort is when you have to come back—' he threw his eyes skyward as if to say *typical* '—and you're always more worn out by then.'

I smiled and rolled my eyes too. 'Ah yes, always the way.'

A valley descent. Rock scramble. Return ascent. Moderate. Got it.

'Enjoy the hike!' he called out, as the door swung closed behind me.

Later, I would think about this conversation, this brief and unremarkable exchange, and how it could have provided some chance to grasp a lifeline. I wondered whether either of us could have, should have, seen the possibility of what lay ahead. What if my checking-in about the trail had been noted more officially? A sign-in sheet, perhaps? Why wasn't there such a check-in system in place at all? And, more to the point, how had I not bothered to check in with anyone? How the hell had it not occurred to me that I should inform someone? *Anyone?* It's the single most valuable rule that all experienced travellers know: tell somebody where you're going, what your plans are, and when you expect to return. I knew that rule.

Whenever I was at home in New Zealand and I picked up the

newspaper and read of visiting travellers who had gone for a walk in the bush and got into trouble – getting lost and injured, or caught out by a sudden change in weather, sparking widespread search parties – I'd sigh sadly and say, 'See, that's why you always tell someone where you're going.' I reckoned I knew better than to be so careless. But *I was careless.* I'd become so comfortable travelling on my own, spending so much time in my own company, and accounting only for myself, that when I drove into the national park that day, I hadn't told my plans to anybody.

It hadn't even crossed my mind.

Instead, I was anticipating nothing more than a day of glorious solitude, a walk in the desert on an established trail to a hidden oasis. As I smiled a cheery goodbye to the ranger in the visitor's centre I could never have foreseen what was going to happen, what would go so terribly, terribly wrong. There is no way I could have known this man almost became the last person I ever spoke to.

The trail to the Lost Palms Oasis begins as it ends, with a cluster of palms. A sort of appetizer, a preview of what's to come. The Cottonwood Oasis is a small group of slender fan palms, marking the trailhead for three different trails: the shortest being a gentle loop around the oasis perimeter, the longest being the one I was about to embark on.

I was not alone at the trailhead. As I locked up the Mini I noticed another vehicle in the car park. A couple about my age were clearly preparing for a hike of their own, zipping up day packs, adjusting their trainers and baseball caps. The woman was swigging water while the man asked her whether they should take sunscreen with them. *Yes, mate*, I thought to myself. The heat of the day was already rising and out here it could hit 40 Celsius. *Slip, Slop, Slap.*

For a moment I wondered whether being late to get started meant I would now be tailing other hikers all day. It wasn't a big deal, there can be an amiable cordiality in meeting other walkers on a hike, but today I was really in the mood for some bona-fide solitude. The very reason I'd chosen a Tuesday morning for this walk was because I figured it would be one of the quietest times in the week to go. At the weekend, the car parks would be full to bursting and the crowds that converge on the trails certainly take the shine off the peace and calm, their presence adding unwelcome blots of synthetic colour to the landscape.

I figured I'd better set off quickly. The other hikers would only be a few steps behind me at this rate. Rucksack on my back, stick in one hand and water bottle swinging from the other, I set off on the trail as it curved around the edge of the oasis, the shadows of the palms passing across my face. I noticed the couple, somewhere off behind me, heading right. They must be walking the shorter Mastadon trail.

I guess I had the Lost Palms trail to myself after all.

Hiking alone is so very different from hiking with other people and you're either someone who's into it or you're not. It's like travelling alone versus not: both are valuable, both are brilliant, but how you engage with the world around you is entirely different. I love to grab a friend, or a few of them, and hit a trail together, but more often than not I go by myself.

And while much of the time this is circumstantial – there isn't usually someone around, or available, to take with me – it's also a deliberate choice. Walking in my own company is one of the best opportunities for being alone with my thoughts and reconnecting with myself. It's only me and the earth beneath my feet, the relief of feeling suddenly insignificant, just another animal on the plains. In solitude, everything is heightened: sounds, scenery, the palpable sense of being right here, right now. Being alone in nature, with only my thoughts and the great wide open, is an utter, immeasurable pleasure. Hiking is my meditation, the liberating space of wilderness is the greatest place in which to clear my mind.

In fact, walking takes me right out of my head altogether. Otherwise I can easily become trapped in it. Locked in there and climbing the walls, slowly going a bit mad. Everyone, I think, has those places or environments that bring them calm and clarity. I can be alone with my thoughts any old place – at home, in bed, in the corner of some coffee shop somewhere – but there's something about being outdoors and away from civilization, on a path, just putting one foot in front of the other, that helps me to metabolize my emotion in a way that nothing else seems to do. Walking alone affords me the time and the space to discard mental clutter, air out my ideas, stretch my emotional legs and simultaneously to breathe, feel a sense of calm and be absolutely, unequivocally present. I can't think of any other instance where I can successfully do that.

These are the conditions in which I feel most content and free. I breathed deeply, in then out, and stopped to read a wooden sign on the side of the track.

LOST PALMS OASIS TRAIL
(CARRY WATER)
3.4 MILES

A jolt of excitement. I was entering my happy place.

It was idyllic walking that morning. The route began with a slow, steady climb up staircases of rock, eventually flattening out to a path along a high dune, the low desert rolling out for miles on all sides. I stopped and rotated slowly on the heels of my boots, taking in the full 360-degree panorama, then taking a video, and photos, to capture it and keep it for ever.

The landscape was magical. Tall, spindly ocotillos stretched their lightning branches up towards the sky, while closer to the ground bulbous red cacti set blots of colour amongst the greens and browns of the squat, twiggy creosote bush that scattered across the rolling, undulating terrain, skirting around the cubist formations of giant boulders that punctured the horizon. I found it fascinating, humbling even, that so much can live and thrive in a place like this.

I felt like I was thriving too. I was surprised to find that since coming to Joshua Tree I hadn't felt lonely. I had been lonely in Canada, but here I felt relieved of that familiar melancholy. Sure, I was getting to know people here, but most of the time was spent in my own company and this somehow felt different than it had in Canada, or back in London. I felt lighter...content. And the ease I was feeling seemed to connect me to the world I wandered in. The previous weekend I'd popped into the local tattoo shop to enquire the cost of an ear piercing and wound up spending more than an hour there, chatting to owners Tom and Gayle, looking through photo albums of their travels to England, and eventually getting the piercing right there after all, because what the hell, we'd all got to know each other, there was a camaraderie now.

I'd also scoured the tiny local bookstore further down the road, its shelves stacked neatly with well-loved tomes, searching for a book my friend Henrietta had recommended to me and I'd been looking for fruitlessly ever since I left London – John Steinbeck's *Travels with Charley*.

'You absolutely need this book,' she'd said, one of the last times I saw her before I left. Drinking whisky from a delicate teacup in her tiny treasure chest of a living room, not one sip ever dislodging her red lipstick, she'd almost admonished me for not having read it.

'*How* have you not read it? You must find it. You'll love it.'

Henrietta was an adventurous soul herself, and she never talked fluff, so I believed her. I hunted for it in used bookstores on my travels across Canada, without any success. But Jean-Paul, who ran the bookstore in Joshua Tree, knew it well and was pretty sure he had a spare copy kicking about at home. 'Let me take a look,' he'd said. 'Come back and see me in a couple of days and I'll have it for you.'

I wasn't used to all this openness. Everywhere I went I felt connections were happening, and in such an easy, natural way. And while it was easy to pin it on this place I had found myself in, I knew it wasn't as straightforward as that. The change was coming from me. I was finally opening up.

An hour and a half in, the trail followed a wash cut through high, sandy banks. A wash is a dried-out riverbed, dug out of silted sand, that becomes a fast-flowing waterway on the rare occasion of heavy rain. They say Joshua Tree averages six inches of rain per year. Suffice to say that most of the time, a wash remains a wash. The path here was much wider than it had been, the landscape almost growing higher around me, branches and boulders throwing shadows across the sand. As I turned each corner, my eyes scanned the path on either side for signs of movement, the various shadowy pockets a likely hangout for snakes.

The wash eventually narrowed and reached a wall of rock, where the path dropped away on the other side by a few feet. I recalled my conversation with the ranger, how he had mentioned that there would be some scrambling as the path descended – this was it. I slipped off my rucksack, leaned the stick against the rock and took a swig of water, preparing myself for the clamber down. It was not an unreasonable drop, but it was a decent one, which made me question whether this trail was fairly categorized as 'moderate'. This part of the trail would certainly be challenging to some. But it didn't feel too difficult for me; I was glad for a challenge. This was why I came for the Lost Palms Oasis, because I wanted a hike that required a little more of me. A moderate level trail. Not too strenuous...Just strenuous enough.

I dropped my rucksack down first, letting it fall with a gentle thud on to the gritty sand, then threw down my water bottle after it. I heard it crack and saw a small piece of the red plastic lid fly off. *Ah, shit.* Clutching the hiking stick tightly in one hand I crouched, slid forward on my backside, and – thud – dropped to my feet in the wash.

There came a pang of regret when I realized the drop had indeed broken my trusty water bottle; the plastic lid with its folding handle had snapped on impact, the handle broken right off at the hinge. A shame, as it was the handle which had made it so easy to carry on hikes, allowing me to swing it effortlessly from a couple of fingers. We'd recently been on some grand adventures, this bottle and I – on hikes and drives and travels...I guessed that was the end of that.

I really shouldn't get sentimental about such things.

It was a habit I started young, forming an emotional attachment to *stuff*. Looking back, I think it was a way to connect myself with things that felt significant. The problem was, as it tends to be when you're a kid, *everything* felt significant. I once carved my initials into my favourite wooden chair in primary school so that I could always select it during assemblies, finding some strange comfort in something constant. On the last day of the school year, when everyone was saying emotional goodbyes, readying themselves to shift gear and become high-schoolers, I was feeling particularly sentimental. And so when it was announced that, thanks to our school fair fundraising efforts, they would be replacing all the assembly chairs over the summer break, I felt no guilt sneaking into the hall, stealing 'my' chair and walking all the way home with it, the wooden backrest clutched to my chest and the legs sticking out in front. I think I lied and told my parents they were giving them away.

I was always collecting things like this. Even into my teens. A broken pen that once belonged to a boy I had a crush on. A chipped wooden doorstop, nicked from the concert venue where I saw Radiohead when I was 15 and slipped into my pocket, because Thom Yorke had trod on it as the band came out to their waiting vehicle.

What I was really collecting was moments. Moments and feelings that I wanted to keep, that were too good to let go of or forget. It was the same reason why I took so many photos. By the time I moved out of home I had a box full of undeveloped film, more than I could afford to get developed. And most of which, had they even survived expiry, would have contained nothing interesting at all.

They say, in psychological terms, that having attachments to possessions is a way of compensating for unreliable attachments in other people. I mean, obviously it's so much easier to cling to *things*. I'd become more aware of my quiet sentimentality towards objects over the years and had tried to work on it. And while I'd never quite shaken the habit entirely, I had become better at recognizing it and letting go.

The water bottle wasn't valuable to me, but I noticed I was lingering on the memories already attached to it. Places I'd been, adventures I'd had. I'd acquired it from a consignment of kitchenware sent in to the magazine where I worked, and from there I had trotted it around Canada, on hikes and drives, only to see it come to its end right here. *Thank you for your service,* I thought wryly, and snapped the lid back on as securely as the cracked plastic would allow. I guess this would be its last hike.

I'll get another one when I get back into town.

And so, with the bottle clutched in one hand and the hiking stick in the other, I carried on through the wide curve of the wash.

Probably less than an hour later, I came to the boulder stack. It must have been about 10 feet to the top, not particularly high, and the trail seemed to disappear beneath it, creeping in between the boulders like a river. I figured this was where more of that aforementioned scrambling must begin.

'...there is a bit of a scramble once you get to the valley...so as long as you're comfortable with climbing over rocks...'

So up I went, stepping up from one rock to the next, tentatively lifting my legs around scraggy branches and brush tucked in amongst them, collecting scratches on my knees, keeping a trepidatious eye out for snakes as I placed fingers and boots into rocky ledges.

From the top of the boulders the valley fell away, rolling away for miles; it was breathtaking. Soaring rocky buttes that rose high to meet the blue sky, irregular patches of open sandy clearing interrupted by piles of monumental boulders, tiny specks of sage-green foliage tucked in the crevices.

The desert never disappoints.

I sat in the cool shade of an overhang, propping the heels of my boots into the rock, catching my breath and having a drink. Now that my bottle was broken, it was going to be a pain in the arse to hold, so I drained the last of the water from it and stashed it in my backpack. One less thing to carry – I would just use the CamelBak from here on in. I adjusted the blue polyurethane bladder so that the drinking tube was attached to my shoulder strap for easy access. I was now a quarter of the way through my water, but I calculated I still had enough to get me there and back.

To carry on from the boulder stack I first had to figure out where the trail continued from the other side – and then how to get down. The path seemed to split into two, winding separately and intermittently through the valley. The first was down to my left. Here the path looked wider, curving around boulders in a wide swoop, but it would be almost impossible to climb directly down to. This side was more than 10 feet up, maybe even double that; way too far to simply drop down, like I had in the wash. The other route, on the opposite side of the stack, was more accessible. It looked like it would take a little more effort to pick my way around rocks, but it would certainly be much easier to get down to, a sturdy descent rather than the sheer drop directly below me. I'd take this route. I'd just have to get myself across these boulders.

Often, the most dangerous moves are the ones that don't feel like it: there are no red flags, no alarm bells. The greater the sense of risk we feel, the more careful we are, ensuring our decisions lean on the side of caution. If you do something frequently enough you naturally become more confident. But confidence is just an absence of fear, or a great ability to ignore it.

The problem with confidence is that it breeds complacency, and as time goes on, not being obstructed by fear becomes our normal, something we start taking for granted. I was doing something really risky, without appreciating that I was, because I was comfortable here, comfortable in this place, and in my solitude. And it made me blind to dangers that should have been obvious. I should have sensed how risky it was to try to cross the boulder stack.

Complacency is the well-trod path towards that classic mantra of fools:

It won't happen to me.

Complacency kills.

All I was thinking about in that moment was how best to cross. It was clear right away that my biggest challenge was a single large, pale-grey boulder, larger than I was, the surface contrastingly smoother than the craggy rocks around it. It was far too wide to simply stretch a leg over, which meant I'd need to step directly on to it. That's where things would require a bit of delicacy. But I had faith in my balance. I had faith in my boots, with their high-quality rubber soles. I felt confident.

Leaning all my weight into my left side, I extended my right leg towards the centre of the boulder and let the inner edge of my boot kiss the face of it, pressing the rubber into a small crevice I could see in the rock. It held.

I gave it a little more of a press. Once again, it seemed to hold. So I gave it some more weight, eventually shifting my body into it, preparing to swing myself to the other side, where the rough rocks offered more grip.

Only...I had been wrong about the foothold.

The moment I gave most of my weight to the rock, I found the crevice I had relied on was not a crevice at all but a mere dimple in the rock, smooth and unforgiving to even a high-quality rubber sole. It was not going to hold me.

Shit. No.

No no no...

Abort mission.

But it was too late to pull back; gravity had now taken over.

And I felt myself start to slide.

It's strange how moments become suspended in time. Everything during those next few seconds happened so fast, yet each movement left a clear and perceptible etch in my memory. My right foot slipping. My left hip leaning hard into the boulder I was sitting on. The desperate flutter as the fingers of my left hand scrabbled for something to hold on to, but found only rock, as flat and smooth as an ocean-worn pebble. My right hand tightly gripping my hiking stick, thrusting it at the boulder beneath me, failing to find traction, failing to slow my momentum. The words 'No no no no!' still beating against my tongue while my brain called a warning to my body: *you are about to get hurt.* The rockface jutted out so that I couldn't see how far down I was going to fall or what I was going to land on – I only knew that falling was inevitable.

All of this seemed to happen so slowly, almost gracefully, yet in real time it was no more than a few desperate seconds. A slide and a brief scuffle of dust.

And with that, I slipped off the edge.

LONDON

My head was killing me. Somebody was hammering on the inside of my skull. BANG. BANG. BANG. I opened my eyes and it took me a good moment or two to figure out what I was looking at. About an inch from my nose appeared the spines of books and wall of wooden boards, which – and this confused me – I seemed to be leaning against. How odd that I would have my cheek pressed against the wall like this, but the instinct to move seemed momentarily fuzzy. The books looked familiar though.

The sound of banging in my head eased slightly, just enough

for me to notice a high-pitched ringing. I kept on staring at the books and the planks, my brain trying to reassemble pieces from my memory, revealing the picture. Finally, the cogs began to turn and recognition clicked on like a fridge light: I was looking at the bottom of my bookshelf.

Which meant I was lying on the floor.

What was I doing on the floor?

I lifted my throbbing head, felt a tug of resistance and heard the sticky sound of my face peeling away from the floorboards, as if it had been glued there. The spot where I'd been laying was covered in a clear puddle of residue. A quick touch of my face revealed a sticky crystallized layer was coating my skin. And then I saw the bottle. Cocktail sugar syrup. It was smashed, tiny glittering shards of glass scattered on the floor, the contents spilled out, and I'd been lying in it.

As I dizzily got to my feet I began to gather a picture of what had happened. I'd got out of bed to go to the bathroom and walked back into my room. The syrup, a random acquisition from a magazine cocktails shoot, had been sitting on top of the little IKEA bookshelf near the foot of my bed. And for some reason I had fainted. While I couldn't remember it happening I knew how the moment would have gone down: I'd have collapsed to my knees, the impact toppling the bottle off the bookshelf and on to the floor, where it smashed. I would have then slumped the rest of the way to the floor, face-first into the syrup and shards of glass.

I patted myself down and assessed the rest of my body; the black silk of my dressing gown was sticky with crystallized syrup. And my hair was glued together in clumps. What a mess. The clock announced 2am. Worried about waking my flatmate, Mara, asleep in her room across the hall, I tiptoed into the bathroom, not even daring to turn the light on lest the tug of the cord made too loud a click. In the darkness I leaned over the sink and attempted to rinse off the sugar that coated my face. The cold water was soothing on my throbbing forehead, but as my fingers moved across my features I felt a thick flap of skin lift away from the side of my nose. My blood ran cold.

Oh my god. My face.

I scurried back to my bedroom and peered in the mirror. My face was a mess of blood and sugar; glass had sliced across one eyebrow, my cheek, my chin, and cut deep into the side of my nose. Panic rose in my guts and I felt my head spin. Might I faint again? I grabbed my phone, tiptoed into the living room, sat myself firmly on the sofa, and called an ambulance.

I was determined not to wake Mara. It was 2am for chrissakes. I went to great lengths to make sure I didn't disturb her, tiptoeing around, dressing in silence, talking quietly to the emergency services, and muting my ringtone so that every time they called to apologize for the delay it wouldn't make a sound.

I had sat alone in the dim light of the living room, trembling gently with shock and the fear of not really understanding what had happened, until the sun began to rise over the blocks of flats across the street. The occasional tear ran down my cheek, moistening the coating of sugar and blood that was stuck to my skin. I was afraid, I realized. Afraid of what happened. By the time the ambulance arrived I'd been sitting there for four hours.

The uniformed responders were apologetic as they checked my pupils – 'Sorry for the wait, Saturday is our busiest night of the week' – and bundled me into the back of the ambulance. Once *en route* to the Royal London Hospital I wrote Mara a text, figuring by now it would be a reasonable enough hour to message her to give her a heads-up as to what had happened, why I'd be gone when she got up and that I wouldn't be able to go to the new food market by the canal like we'd planned. To apologize if the sound of voices had woken her up, but an ambulance crew had stopped by.

This was exactly my brand of casual pragmatism. I had this. No need to fuss. And really, I was mortified by my own drama, with no desire to make it anyone else's. This was my mess and now I was fixing it.

It's so ridiculous when I think about it now. Mara was not just my flatmate, she was my friend. And she had, quite justifiably, been furious with me, once she'd woken to my texts and learned that I'd secretly snuck off to hospital with a bloody face.

'WTF!? Why the hell didn't you wake me? I would have taken you!'

Naturally I'd waved her away with the usual, 'Thanks, I know. But it's OK! I'm fine.'

I'm fine.

I'd been saying that for so long that it was a subconscious impulse. I'm fine. I got this. I not only said it to everyone around me, but to myself. Did I actually believe it? And how often had it been true? 'I'm fine' was a mask I had become so comfortable wearing that I'd long forgotten I was still hiding behind it. And that's what I was doing. Hiding. Hiding the parts of me that were weak, and vulnerable, driven by a potent cocktail of fear and shame.

The doctor scheduled a couple more tests but, for the most part, could see no cause for the black-out. 'Have you been feeling stressed out lately?'

I waved away the suggestion. I wasn't someone who got stressed out.

Was I?

I'd returned home that afternoon, my nose taped up, little cuts dashed across my face and my hair still full of sugar, and my first thought was relief that Mara and I could still make the food market.

'Come on, let's go get coffee and donuts!' I called from my bedroom, as I yanked on some fresh clothes, the sugar-coated ones discarded in the laundry basket.

Mara thought I was crazy. I mean, I certainly looked the part.

'Are you sure? If I'd just got out of hospital, I'd be going straight to bed,' she said, shaking her head.

'After the night I've just had, I *need* coffee and donuts,' I replied.

I might have been sleep-deprived, mildly concussed and looked like I fell face-first into a cat, but I couldn't see any reason why we shouldn't still go.

We might as well get on with things.

'Really, I'm fine. C'mon.'

So we wandered down to the canal, as if nothing had happened. As we sat on a bench on the edge of the canal clasping our cardboard cups of coffee, Mara still seemed to be getting her head around the peculiarity of my decisions.

'I still can't believe you didn't just wake me up,' she said.

'Yeah. I was actually trying very hard to make sure I didn't.'

'Jeez,' she said, gently chuckling with bewilderment, 'you really find it hard to need people.'

That was it, wasn't it. The notion of waking my friend, putting her out, and ultimately being on the receiving end of assistance, was something I had instinctively avoided. Forget the fact I'd passed out and almost sliced my nose off – I had a bigger question. Why *was* is it so hard for me to need anybody? Why was my first instinct to fend for myself? Also, did this have anything to do with me feeling down lately?

I suppose I'd misled myself by thinking that if I could do everything alone, if I didn't need anyone else, I was strong. But there's nothing strong about hiding your fears, nothing noble about not asking for help. I had this idea of who I was and that the way I dealt with things came from some kind of strength, when in truth, I was merely hiding. Building walls that allowed me to control whether I let anything in or out. Hardly the actions of someone fearless. The irony is not lost on me that it took waking up coated in sugar to learn that I was sugarcoating my own emotions.

What I was only now waking up to was that yes, I was capable of fending for myself, but that didn't mean I *had* to. And the more I pressed on like this, the more I carried on determinedly dealing with problems on my own, the more likely I was to crumble. Other people want to help. They really do. And by letting them help – by asking them to – you are creating an opportunity. You are inviting them in. We come from a history of tribes; the very nature of our species means we thrive best in a village community. We are designed to pull together.

Connection is very much a necessity for survival.

Since I realized all this, I've wondered what it was that drove me to avoid help all this time – not so much help in the professional sense, but rather letting my emotional burdens be shared, my logistical challenges be eased, my screw-ups and fears and vulnerabilities revealed. In the first instance I think it came from guilt: I didn't want to put anybody out. I didn't want to be a burden. And I guess if I needed someone, then they might need me back, and then what mess would I be in? To be needed?

I was afraid of letting anyone in, but boy, it got lonely in there.

———

I was airborne for about half a second before hitting the ground, landing about 20 feet below the edge of the rock face.

It was no small miracle that I had landed, not on one of the many boulders or clusters of rocks that surrounded me, but in a small, flat clearing, although piles of large boulders hemmed me in. I was hidden from anyone's view.

Behind me was the stack I had fallen from and a couple of feet to my right was a high, overhanging boulder with a long, rounded tip that stuck out like a thumb. At my feet, more stacks of rocks, and to my left – the only side not completely walled in – the trail I had seen from above seemed to lead out around the rocky terrain. In the distance beyond that it reached a towering red cliff.

The left side of my pelvis had taken most of the impact; shattering, pieces disconnected, leaving me unable to raise my body below the waist. It was like pressing down on a faulty pedal bin. The futility of my situation hit me hard. I couldn't move, the lack of signal meant I couldn't call the emergency services... I couldn't tell a single living soul that I was here. I tried sending texts to a few people in the hope they might, somehow, by some chance, get through – a twitch of a signal coming through on the breeze. Anything. My fingers shook as I frantically tapped out a message, for once in my life the programmed habit of capitalization and punctuation being scrambled by panic:

```
I've fallen and smashed my pelvis and cant
walk need help — lost palms oasis
```

But each time, the little red exclamation mark screamed out: Not Delivered.

I combed my iPhone extensively, desperately, looking for any sort of app or method of communication that might work. Scrolling through settings, I found something called Emergency SOS and immediately stabbed at it with my finger. This is precisely what I need! Emergency SOS! Thank god, I *knew* there had to be something like this installed, how can we have all this technology and not have something for a situation like this? My heart raced, excited, as I read that it will alert the emergency services with my location and send texts to my allocated emergency contacts.

OK. Emergency contacts.

It didn't even matter who I contacted, but I hurriedly lined up a few people to reach out to – my parents, the people I'd met in Joshua Tree, Caroline back in Toronto...

Then I activated the SOS function. Texts were sent out to each person I'd allocated:

```
Emergency SOS — I have made an emergency
call from this approximate location. You
```

are receiving this message because I have
listed you as an emergency contact.

The little red exclamation mark popped up again.

Not Delivered.

I tried again.

Not Delivered.

No! You've got to be kidding me!

The emergency SOS function requires phone signal.

My heart sank into my stomach. All I could hope now was that another hiker would come by today and find me. That was it – that was all I had left to cling to. I wondered how long it would be before someone else walked the trail. How busy did it get during the week? The voice in my head answered that question for me but I chose not to hear it.

Was there really nothing else I could do?

I opened my maps and found I could still access my GPS in my downloaded maps. I could at least see where I was. There was the Lost Palms Oasis trail, a tiny dotted line in a vast expanse of nothing. And there was me, the little blue dot.

Except the little blue dot was not on the trail.

It was somewhere below it.

No. That can't be right. I can't be there.

I pinched my fingers against the screen and zoomed in to get a clearer look. There had to be an error. But that wiggly broken line was definitely the trail; I could see the words 'Lost Palms Oasis' at the very tip of it. And I was not on it. Not even close. According to the map I was out by at least a mile, maybe more. I stared at the screen, feeling the cold prickles of horror run down my neck.

I'm not on the trail.

Somewhere along the way I had taken a wrong direction... Instead of heading towards the palms, I had turned off and veered south. Left the trail. Headed into complete nothing. The path I thought was a continuation of the trail was also nothing. Only desert.

I stared at the screen again, breathing '*No no no...*'

It hit me, then.

No one was going to be coming by. No one.

That last remaining line of opportunity to get out of here, the one I'd been clutching so tightly to, was gone. I was nowhere near a trail, and nobody was going to pass by this place and find me.

I howled, not a scream for help but a sound like a wounded animal, letting it trail off until there was no more air in my lungs. My heart felt like it might sink right through my chest and into the dirt below me. I felt the tiny stones sticking sharply into my back.

It was likely I would die here.

This was it, wasn't it?

I was going to die in the desert, and it was not going to be quick. I was going to watch it happen. And I was going to be alone. Nobody had noticed I wasn't around, and nobody knew I was out here, trapped. In death I would finally understand what loneliness really was. And the world would go on turning without me.

It was like the wind had been kicked out of me.

Hot tears pricked my eyes.

I didn't want to die, there was too much ahead.

Please. I am not ready. I am really not ready.

It's the strangest feeling, suddenly knowing how your story is going to end. The brain fights against it, denial and pragmatism locked in a violent wrestle. I was trying to absorb the reality of my own death and found my mind could not fully grapple with it, not yet, and instead it began to conjure up pictures of the aftermath. Thoughts turned to my parents. I pictured my mum being told that I was dead – although how does anyone really know how a scene like that would go? All I could be sure of is that it would begin with a phone call. An American number connecting through to New Zealand. The black cordless phone on the kitchen counter, sunlight strewn across the little table with its round bowl of plump lemons that my mum and stepdad always had growing in abundance. My imagination saw my mother picking up the phone, heard her voice as she absorbed the blow of the information, processing it, trying to keep a handle on the worst news one can get. I imagined her being quiet, wanting to be alone, maybe disappearing down the bottom of the garden with a cigarette and dealing with tears alone, away from anyone else. But howling on the inside while handling this on her own. It was a response I understood. It is what I would have done.

I imagined Mum calling my dad. I could see his face, hear his voice... but my mind couldn't fill in the emotional gaps of that conversation. Dad was always the joker. My father and I co-existed on a plane of humour and frivolity; we didn't engage in the emotional stuff. When had I ever seen him cry?

We're not a family that does crying very well. We don't wear our emotions where people can see them.

My younger brother Chris was the same. He and I could talk so frankly and openly with each other, but that was talk.

Matter-of-fact. I valued this talk, though. We'd reached that magic point in sibling adulthood where we'd become not only allies, but friends. *I'd meant to text him tonight,* I'd thought. We'd taken a trip to Iceland not too long ago, just the two of us, both awed by the landscape. The whole time I'd been out here I kept thinking how much he would have loved the desert. One of my parents would have to phone him in Sydney.

My mind shifted to friends calling one another, passing on the news. Who would hear it from whom? How would they react? One by one, I was conjuring up scenes of the people in my life learning about my death. Not out of any conceit – but because this was the only way it could feel real to me. I could not get my head around the concept of my own death, but through the eyes of those I cared about, I could start to see it. Like squinting at an eclipse through a sheet of kitchen foil.

And how long, I wondered, would it take for the news to reach anyone? How long, in fact, before they figured out what had happened to me? What I had done? Which would happen first? Would someone, somehow, come across my remains by chance and alert the authorities? Or would my absence be noticed and then, eventually, my body would somehow be found out here? Or perhaps my body would never be located at all.

At this point there was little I could do but run through the what-ifs and the how-mights. What else could I do?

I could scream.

Screaming felt like the right thing to do in this situation, but I was at least a mile off the trail, which may or may not have someone on it, so who the hell was going to hear me? I couldn't tell whether the sound of my screams even made it past the boulders that towered over me. I screamed as loud as I could, sending it cannoning from the centre of my gut, then paused to listen, to hear if I could get a sense of where the scream landed. While there was a faint echo, there was no way of knowing just how far it reached.

I screamed anyway. It helped to do something. It was a dilemma, really, whether to do it or not, and how long to keep it up for at a time. I screamed as loudly and for as long I could, but it made my mouth dry up, left my throat raw and raspy, and I didn't know if there was even any point.

But a little voice in the back of my mind kept clinging to the idea that what if – somehow – one scream happened to reach far enough that a hiker was near enough to just catch the sound as carried on the breeze? What if they then had the foresight to investigate it? What if that one scream turned out to be the singular thing that saved my life?

God I was desperate. All I could do was hang on to the what-ifs.

I had no other way of signalling my whereabouts, had there been anyone to signal to. I looked around me. My sunglasses had landed a couple of metres to my left, too far for me to reach. Maybe I could pull them towards me with the hiking stick. I looked around for it. Where had the stick gone? It had been in my hand as I'd fallen, but I couldn't see it anywhere.

Shit, shit, shit.

It couldn't have gone far. It fell with me. Where did it go? Nothing to my left, or my right, and nothing by my feet. So what if...

I reached my hand up behind my head to touch the rock – there was a low, smooth shelf there. Opening the camera on my iPhone, I held it high and scanned the area around me, giving me a lay of the land. And – yes! There it was. I could see it. The stick had landed on the shelf of rock behind my head. If only I could get it. And then I had an idea. I pulled my t-shirt out of my rucksack and, holding one corner of it, I whipped it behind my head. I heard the stick rattle against the rock. I whipped it again. Another reassuring rattle. *Come on. Come onnnn.*

After a few attempts, the shirt flicked the stick over the shelf and onto my head, and I snatched it up, the feel of it in my grip making me feel a little more empowered, a little bigger. In it, I had an extension of myself. Using the stick, I was able to drag my sunglasses within reach and then, one by one, I pulled my things around me. Having them close making me feel safer. Equipped. Even though there was little any of my belongings could do to save me from my own awful predicament.

Above me a hawk had begun to circle – a dark arrow hovering way up high, wings outstretched, scanning the canyon. I watched it. Was it watching me too? Fear ran cold through my blood as I considered where I now fell in the chain of desert life. *Potential prey.*

Really, I was a needle in a haystack. How could anyone find me? Even if I died here…? What if, by the time anybody does stumble upon this place, and they find my body, my broken bones are long picked clean by the vultures and the animals and the baking sun, and they don't know who I am or what happened? I'd heard stories, real-life stories of remains found in the dirt out here. What if I become one of them? One of those nameless, gruesome and heartbreaking tales of a dead hiker found years after their loved ones reported them missing?

Oh god. I don't want to die, I really don't want to die.
Panic was going to get the better of me if I let it.
Breathe. Just breathe.
I breathed in deeply, slowly, counting to five, letting air fill my lungs, remembering the meditation apps I'd tried countless times during bouts of anxiety and insomnia. Every breath chipped away at my rising panic, but the expanding of my torso made the agonizing pain burn through my body, the pieces of bone feeling hot like coal on a fire, forcing me to cry out, imploring me to keep still.

My hands were shaking.

I want them to know what happened. Whoever finds me needs to know.

I would leave a message. Just in case. I wiped the grit and dust from my face with the end of my bandana. My hands were still shaking. I didn't quite know what to say; I didn't want this to be a goodbye message – I was not ready for that...but I don't want it to not be a goodbye message either.

Oh god.

I could hear my brain make its usual push–pull between strength and vulnerability, this battle so much a part of me that I already knew who would win it.

You need to say something.
Let's not be too dramatic.
Except you might die.
And this might be the last thing you say to anyone.
But oh god, I am not good at emotions.
Don't be pathetic.
Stay strong.

I really don't know what to say...
Or how I should say it...
But I have to say something.
I pressed record and let the words fall out.

[video] *I did a dumb thing! I was scrambling and I fell down*
into this hole, and I think I've shattered my pelvis, and I can't get
signal, and I'm screaming for help and – oh fuck, I'm so scared –
I'm trying not to panic...But you know if I die here, this is what's
happened, I've just been a stupid idiot. But I love you all and you
know that. And I'm out here because I'm 'living my best life'! But
I'm not going to give up hope yet...There's always hope.

As I stopped the recording I felt foolish, and scared, and then
pragmatism kicked in. It occurred to me...If I didn't get out of
here, how would anyone see that message? Nobody would know
it was on my phone, and anyway, how could they access it? I
recalled a friend of someone I knew, a girl close to my age, killed
in a terrible accident on her travels, and not even her closest family
members were able to get into her iPad once it was returned to
them, unable to retrieve her photos, anything.

Then there was the matter of conserving the battery, which
was already slipping under 50 per cent. In the back of my mind I
still held on to a far-fetched hope that a signal might get through
somehow; perhaps some miraculous shift in the stratosphere.
Who the hell knew...I had no real understanding of cellular
technology, but ignorance left my imagination wide open to the
possibility that something, somehow, might connect. The idea of
my phone going flat made my heart stop.

So that wasn't going to work. My phone wouldn't do.

But I had a digital camera.

Anyone could access that.

I held my camera inside my hat, the lens pointing towards me, and pressed record.

[video] *This is not where I expected to end up – with a shattered pelvis...in the desert. I might die here and I'm really scared that that's the case and I don't know what to do...I can't get signal out here. And I call for help and no one's out here. This is the stupidest thing I've ever done. I can't move...Fuck...I'm trying to keep covered from the sun, trying to ration my water...There's a hawk up there, fuck...I'm so scared, I need to get out of here. And in case I don't, I just want to say I love you all – I love my family, I love you. And my friends, who have been family to me. To all of you, you know who you are, you're good people. I love you.*

I was rambling. Still holding back. There was that little voice in my head that was still shaming me in my moment of vulnerability. Even here, exposed in the glaring face of my own potential demise, I held back. I didn't know if anyone would see this, but what if I got rescued, god willing, and the video was watched – it might seem so...melodramatic. Weak. It's really hard to come out from behind the curtain and be vulnerable and the instincts that had seen me through my entire life were not about to budge so quickly. Wasn't this the big mistake I had been making all along? Putting on my brave face?

Harden up. Just get on with it.

And maybe it didn't matter. Perhaps nobody would see the

message anyway. I might still get out of here and nobody would have to know I'd ever recorded it.

God, I hoped so.

The heat pressed down hard, and simply bearing its weight was soul-sapping work, physically exhausting, even though I was barely moving. There was no way to know what temperatures I was up against, but at this time of year it could reach over 40 Celsius. And this was certainly how hot it felt. I had been using my hat as a shield against the glare, holding it aloft with one arm between myself and the sun like some jaunty eclipse, blocking the burn from my face and upper body. But it was a paltry defence against the wall of oven-heat coming down on me.

I squinted into the mesh of the hat. Through narrowed eyes I could make out the sun, a glowing blur of bluish white. My nemesis. My eyes focused instead on the tag on the inside of my hat band. It was from Marks & Spencer. I remembered when I'd bought it about a year ago, in the men's department of course, and it was still a size large. I'd picked it up ahead of a work trip to Fez, in Morocco – which was, ironically, the last time I'd felt this kind of heat.

I was sent there to write about the food, talking to local people, eating what they were eating, watching them cook, and make, and create, with hands more skilful than anything I ordinarily witnessed in the digital world. I drank in their stories, while travelling, as always, with the duelling emotions of journalism: the utter lightness of joy in the fact I got to do this for a living, and the weighty ball and chain of self-doubt. Every work trip I made felt like a gift, but one that could be taken away from me. As if it might be my last. I wished I hadn't felt that way. I wished

I hadn't needed reassurance that I was meant to be there. I wish I had learned how to own my abilities without apology. Instead, I'd accepted that self-doubt was par for the course. The rent I paid.

One extra upside to this trip, though, was the rare opportunity to take a guest, and I'd brought my friend Telli with me. We were bunked up in a small twin room of an intimate, elaborate riad on the crumbling rim of the ancient medina. Every morning at dawn the hundreds of birds that filled the orange trees in the central garden would burst into song in pin-point unison – it made me think of an arena of football fans in suspenseful silence witnessing a winning goal.

Between interviews, Telli and I would wander the ancient, labyrinthine medina, finding relief in the shadows of the covered souks, busy with locals selecting pastel-pink pomegranates and stubbly, yellow prickly pears. We'd stop at every fountain we passed to soak our cotton scarves under the splashing water, draping them around our necks for relief. God, I could almost feel it, the pleasantness of cool, damp fabric on hot skin. I longed for that now.

But all I had was the hat. And it wasn't quite cutting it out here, in the desert. There was no shade, no cover, no fountains. Just the hat. A thin layer of woven papery straw.

While it did provide some shade for my upper half, my legs continued feeling the relentless burn. I'd unfolded my national park map and awkwardly, given the position I was in, tried to spread it out and drape it over my legs. This offered little respite. It couldn't cover all of me. The heat still got in, searing the exposed patches of my skin like the lick of a flame; I could feel where there was any chink in the paper, the sun creeping in and burning any accessible patches of skin.

Sunscreen. I needed sunscreen. Thankfully, I had packed a tube of SPF60 in my first-aid kit, forgetting I'd already tossed another one in the rucksack the night before – I couldn't have been more grateful to be so well stocked. I was going to need it. Since I couldn't sit up or reach my legs to apply the lotion, the hiking stick would come in useful here. It had, in a way, become my arms, an extension of my body, and I quickly realized I'd have been lost without it. Smothering the thick, white lotion over the knob at the end of the stick I was able to awkwardly smear it over the tops and sides of my shins and my knees. There was instant relief in applying the lotion to my hot skin, but I knew I would have to keep reapplying to fend off the burn.

The bandana I'd borrowed from the house was laid over my chest and my spare t-shirt was draped over my thighs and knees so that, along with the map over my shins, as much of my body was as covered as possible. I had to make constant readjustments, as slight, hot breezes shifted the cover-ups and as the sun moved throughout the day and found new angles from which to reach my skin beneath them.

It also occurred to me that I smelled. A few hours lying here in the dirt and I already reeked of something sweet and musty, of piss and sunscreen and sweat. I couldn't help thinking about coyotes – imagining them lifting their noses to the air, picking up my scent and trotting in my direction. Seeing that coyote earlier that morning was sure a sign as any that they were around.

Hygiene was something I would need to manage. More than a mere boost to the morale – keeping clean seemed like self-defence.

My bladder had been thrown into some sort of shock of its

own and I didn't feel like I had full control over it at first. I had experienced one or two small accidents, which happened as if the lower half of my body had become independent of the rest. I had to try and keep myself as clean and dry as possible. At first, the idea was to try and collect it directly with the water bottle, but I couldn't get it through the leg of my denim shorts. Since I'd long since finished the paracetamol in my small jar of Tylenol, I had this small, empty container, which proved the right size to catch the urine so I could then tip it into the bottle. Even then, every attempt was a wrench on my body; reaching down tensed muscles in my core, agitating the broken parts of me. It also wasn't easy peeing into a small jar while lying on my back, and often I made a mess of it, but it was the best I could do.

The reason I was collecting my urine at all was because the alternative – simply tossing the contents off to the side – seemed more problematic and likely to attract animals. Surely that would be like hanging an olfactory banner: HERE IS MY SCENT, COME AND FIND ME! In that situation, it just felt like a sensible idea to contain it.

Collecting it in the bottle meant I could see the colour of my urine and it looked very dark. Almost reddish in tone. Oh god, was there blood in my urine? Had I damaged my bladder? I had no way of knowing what was going on in my insides right now; my body was wracked with enough pain to cover a multitude of problems. I hoped like hell there wasn't any internal bleeding. In any case, there was nothing I could do about it.

I gave myself a crude wipe down with the roll of toilet paper I'd brought with me, then stashed the dirty wads in my lunchbox – now relegated to the role of rubbish bin – sealing the lid tight.

I slathered my stick of deodorant under my arms and across my belly and rubbed my hands with liquid sanitizer, its medicinal alcohol tang sweet in my nostrils. Of course I still stank, but hopefully if an animal picked up my scent it would acknowledge something more sterile, more obviously human, and hopefully less appealing.

Coyotes aren't really interested in humans, preferring to keep out of one's way. But they are also bold creatures, strutting through front yards like nobody's business, and everyone I knew in the area who had dogs and cats kept them fenced in or indoors, lest they get swiftly plucked by a hungry coyote (or a bird of prey). Adult humans, on the other hand, were too big and not of interest to a wild dog.

Of course, this is all very well when you're going about a normal day. I'd never considered coyotes to be a threat to me, but my perspective was completely different now I was way out here in the wilderness, so far from civilization, flat on my back and unable to move. I was exposed and vulnerable to anything and everything. Who knew what a coyote might do?

The weekend before, I'd been sitting at Mesa Bar, a dive bar in the barren outskirts of the Homestead Valley, about a half-hour drive into the high desert north of Joshua Tree. I'd developed a real soft spot for the place, the curiousness of its remoteness and its off-beat regulars. A squat, concrete building set among the rolling dunes and soft, sandy roads, it wasn't somewhere you'd merely stumble across. Inside, the place was dim and dusty, even on a bright afternoon, with the few windows that ran along one side shuttered to keep out the desert sun. It offered the requisite pub features – pool tables and cash jukebox – but the greatest draw was its U-shaped bar. Pulling up a stool at the bar was an unspoken invitation for anyone else who happened to be sitting around it to converse with you. I enjoyed some kind of thrill in the potluck of conversation, never knowing who you would end up talking to, and the laid-back anticipation of seeing who would wander in next. It tended to be a mixture of grizzled old locals, road-hardened eccentrics and curious travellers who'd heard of the place via word of mouth and wanted to see it for themselves.

The other bonus of drinking at Mesa Bar was one of the friends I'd made in Joshua Tree worked shifts there. Alison and her husband Bryan were a couple of free and easy souls who worked in hospitality and they'd been drawn to the ease and quiet of the desert in much the same way that it appealed to me.

When Natalie had set up introductions for me with some of the folks she had met out here I'd felt initial hesitation in being expected to meet people. *It's easier to occupy my own little space. Why complicate it?* I could feel myself retreating into old, harmful habits, but I didn't come here to shrink into that London bubble and keep people out. I would never find anything in there! I had to change this bullshit behaviour once and for all – I wanted to be outward facing again. So I stepped out of the bubble and in the process made new friends. In fact, I never anticipated just how much I would connect with these people and how quickly. The difference it makes when you come out from behind the wall.

Alison and I had bonded over a shared taste in music and keenness for hiking trails. The Sunday morning before my trip to the oasis, the two of us had been for a hike down Hondo Wash. Parking her van on the side of the sandy trail, we'd continued on foot, searching for animal tracks and interesting rocks and identifying the hollow sun-dried shells of desert gourds.

She was working a shift at the bar from midday so we'd set off early, getting ahead of the heat, and afterwards she invited me back to her house for breakfast. We sat outside her front door, facing the cactus garden and dusty sweep of the yard, discussing the visceral grief we'd each felt when David Bowie and Tom Petty had died. Alison told me how she and Bryan had lived in Portland, Oregon, for a while, but had never really felt things stick for them there.

'It was weird, people were so reluctant to let new people in,' she told me. 'After a while we had enough.'

They bought this house here in the desert, and never looked back. Like me, she'd longed to escape the city life to get closer to the outdoors. This was their idea of balance too.

'You should come by the bar later and hang out,' Alison said.

'You bet.'

It was business as usual that day at Mesa Bar, old-timers propping up the bar and various characters tying up loose conversations on their way out the door. A barefooted couple in their late sixties had just been to a weekend music festival – 'Oh lord, Neil Young was awesome, but Roger Waters came on and totally bummed everyone out...Like, we don't want politics, man, we just want to have a good time' – and were now gathering their two dogs that had been sauntering around between the bar stools. I'd been chatting to Alison between orders when a couple of old bearded bikers ambled in, one a local and the other his oldest friend from way back. Conversation was struck, as per the custom, and somehow – because it's impossible to follow the trajectory of subjects in a place like Mesa Bar – we got to talking about coyotes.

I'd only been at Nat and Lou's house a couple of nights when I first heard the coyotes. A choir of yipping, just outside the window. I'd never heard a coyote before, yet I knew immediately that's what it was. Just like the first time I heard foxes mating in London, a blood-chilling sound like a woman being disembowelled. Natalie and I had both heard them, the two of us tapping on the wall that separated our bedrooms, comforting each other.

The sound of coyotes, though, was nothing like that. It was thrilling, but ethereally beautiful. A chorus of yipping, the kind of sound that could accompany a celebratory dance around a fire. I kicked back my bedclothes and scrambled to my knees, pulling back the curtain and peering into the darkness in the hope that I might see them. They sounded close enough for me to open the window, reach out and touch them. But it was pitch black, no light anywhere to help my eyes in their search. I wondered how well coyotes were at throwing their voices. After that, I heard the coyotes every few nights. And when I did, I would always look for them. Not once did I see them, but I revelled in the sound…it made my veins tingle in some strange, wild way, holding me in the here and now.

'I hear them a lot at night,' I told the men at the bar. 'I just wish I saw more of them. I guess they don't like people much, huh?'

'You gotta be careful with coyotes,' said the one nearest me, who smelled faintly of leather and petrol, in a way that wasn't unpleasant. I noticed he pronounced it ky-oats.

'My neighbour's daughter, just out here—' he pointed to somewhere in the near distance, '—was out on the trail bike and she had three ky-oats show up. She took off and they followed after her. At least half a mile. They've got fearless round here now, they've got used to people.' He took a gulp of his beer. 'Never know what they're gonna do, those ky-oats.'

I thought about all this as I lay there on my back in the canyon, feeling pretty damned vulnerable. If coyotes were bold enough, and desperate enough, I would be easy pickings. All I had was a stick I could swing, and that only to a limited degree, and that was it. That was all I could do.

That, and keeping myself clean. Right now, maintaining a level of personal hygiene felt like a kind of reassurance. And hell, I would take whatever reassurance I could get.

There was also the concerning issue of my clothing being damp. Not only was this grossly unpleasant, I thought about what this might do to me physically – say, a rash, or an unwelcome infection – and how uncomfortable that would be on top of everything else. I had to keep my skin as dry as I could.

There wasn't a hell of a lot I could do but, at the very least, I could remove my underwear. The black nylon briefs that clung to my body were already one more obstacle to contend with when trying to pee into the Tylenol jar and, not being in direct sun, they weren't drying out at all. So, I'd get rid of them. I just had to figure out how. In my present predicament the only way I was going to get them off was to cut them, and I didn't have a knife.

Well, I did. I just hadn't brought it with me. I thought about my shiny new Swiss Army knife, dark red and gleaming steel, still tucked in the pocket of my hold-all, where I'd put it for safekeeping. It had been a gift from my London friends on my last birthday. We had spent the day drinking and grazing on stall food down at Maltby Street market, perched among the antique furniture and gin distillers, followed by dinner at a restaurant among the railway arches. And those of us still present later in the evening had rounded off the day with a stroll to Borough Market for gelato. God, that really had been a good day. And on top of that, it had been such a thoughtful present.

'It's something portable but practical,' Telli had teased. 'Can you guess?'

My friends had long been aware of my growing plans to head off into the Canadian wilderness, on my grand adventure, and had pooled together for something I would be able to use. Something precisely for – and the irony was not lost on me – a situation just like this one.

My friends. I thought of them one by one, picturing their faces, hearing their voices. Fabiana, with her megawatt grin, one of the last friends I saw before I boarded that plane to Toronto. 'Goodbyes are only temporary for the important people,' she'd said. My friends were my second family – when I received my British citizenship, Fabi and Telli had been my guests at the ceremony, applauding. And on my last London afternoon the three of us had met for one final weekend coffee catch-up. I had been frantically busy packing...but some rituals are sacred. *My friends.* Rich and Seb and the boys: my brothers from another mother. The friendly piss-taking and the convivial ease of their company. I'd kept so many of them in the dark. Rich had taken me for a goodbye drink shortly before I left London, when I finally let on to him how I'd been feeling all this time. And what had pushed me to leave. He'd had no idea. And as he sat there and listened, signalling to the sommelier to just bring the whole bottle, I wondered why I had kept all this so quiet even from the people closest to me. I guess I wanted them to see me in a certain way; afraid of not being as likeable, as fun to be around, if I revealed this part of me.

I hoped my friends knew how much they meant to me. And I realized, with an ache in my heart, that none of them would have even noticed I'd disappeared. Comments on Instagram – that was the tenuous means with which we kept in touch. WhatsApp messages were so rare and occasional that my silence would go unobserved by all of them.

I was annoyed that I hadn't brought the knife, but it also made me feel terribly sad.

The sharpest implement I had on me was the tweezers in my first-aid kit. Useful in case I stepped on a cholla cactus and needed to remove the painful spines – I'd already done this once and the burning pain was still fresh in my memory. Cholla are prickly little bastards with fine spines that seem to leap into the nearest piece of exposed flesh and cause a lot of cursing. One of the main reasons you don't go outside in bare feet round here.

Could I tear through the material of the underwear with the tweezers? Unfastening my shorts, I pierced the material of my briefs with the sharp point and spent the next half an hour or so hacking away at them, head raised as far as I could to supervise as I stabbed and ripped all the way along one side, tearing at it with my hands, and then working on the other. I tugged the fabric out from under me – a few tentative pulls at first, then a hard yank and a painful yelp as my pelvis took a shunt – and they were free. I balled them up and stuffed them in the Tupperware box with the rest of my garbage. It felt strangely liberating. And a little breezy.

I'm going commando in the desert!

My shorts were still a little damp but at least my skin could now get more air. This in itself was another small sense of achievement, even if tiny. Even if it was pointless.

I'd take every small victory where I could.

Except out here, it was a case of one step forward, one step back. For each obstacle I tackled, another seemed to creep in. A few moments later a sudden gust of wind blew in through the canyon, as if from nowhere, and stole my map – snatched up from my legs and tossed between the opening in the boulders to my left. I heard the map cling to a rock just out of view, flapping sadly like a wounded bird. I was once again exposed to the burn of the sun. Now, with the map lost in the canyon, it was unbearable. And without protection I could do nothing but lie there, flat on my back, and burn.

As I strained my neck to try to figure out where the map had gone to, a couple of sharp stones shifted beneath me and dug painfully into my shoulder blade. I could do nothing about it – anyway, in terms of pain, there was already plenty of it, and far greater than jabs in my back.

My right hand reached for my rucksack and yanked out the spare map, the one I'd brought by mistake – a happy accident – and, after a few failed attempts to shake the thing out to a full spread, I managed to cover my shins again. This time I took the precaution of weighing it down by lying my hiking stick diagonally across my legs. I couldn't afford to lose this map – without it, I'd have nothing else to protect the lower half of my body.

Holding up the hat was proving a strain; I alternated arms as each one quickly tired. I tried placed the hat on top of the stick instead but holding the stick upright while lying down was almost as exhausting and made it much harder to control the precise position of the hat. One tiny movement of the stick and the sun would blaze down on my face. I needed an extra pair of arms. And anyway, I needed the stick to keep my map down. I wasn't sure how I could keep this up.

Meanwhile, I could hear the missing map rustling with the slightest breeze. It made me jumpy. My senses were on high alert and any small noise became an animal. A predator. Something wandering through the canyon, about to stroll through the boulders and into view. If that actually happened I'd be laughably easy prey: flat on my back, unable to move, cornered inside my enclosure of rock.

Lying there in the canyon I tried not to dwell on the might've been and the never was, but it's difficult not to. The sorrow and the self-pity crept in anyway. I found myself considering all the various chapters of this life I had lived: the places I'd been and the people I'd met.

The people I'd been.

I thought of my life in chapters, full of lives lived. The insecure self-assuredness of my teens. The chapter with the bad boyfriend. The hedonistic London years of my twenties. The chapter with the good boyfriend. The introspective London years of my thirties. The countries I'd travelled to. The people I'd met, conversations had and lessons learned. Scenes and moments drifted through my head like a revolving studio backdrop. The jobs I'd had. God, *so many jobs*. The triumphs, the many, tiny triumphs on the road to doing what I actually loved for a living, which was writing. And what's more, writing about travel. Glimpses of travels flickered through my memory: a New York autumn day strolling through Central Park, eating sea urchins on the back of a boat in the Icelandic ocean, drinking beer in a tiny pinxos bar crammed with exuberant post-football Spaniards...

I'd seen and done so much. I'd really had a great life, hadn't I? I had no right to feel anything but grateful for what I'd crammed in to my 35 years. And it's funny, when you think about the tiniest details you once worried about – agonizing over my crooked teeth; the regular guilt of skipping the gym; fretting over an outfit; stressing over that thing I said once and wished I hadn't; worrying about never having any savings; the crushing anxiety of fucking up at work; the fear of failure, and of never being good enough. It didn't matter.

None of it actually mattered.

Being here and looking back, of course I asked myself whether I had any regrets.

Did I?

No. Not really.

Regret is such a strong word. All my mistakes and poor choices and bad behaviours might not be things I'm proud of, and there is a lot I would like to have not done...but they shaped me. How could I regret the times I'd fallen when they'd taught me how to get up stronger and stand more firmly on my own feet?

I didn't regret not bringing the pocket knife. That was a mistake.

I didn't regret coming on this hike. The fall was an accident.

Making mistakes, and failing, and making decisions that didn't work out as expected, were part of life. I could not regret those things because they were marks of having lived.

Regret, as far as I was concerned, was the stuff you could not forgive yourself for.

And I knew then, there was one thing. I thought about the amount of time I spent – that I wasted – sitting in my room pissing about on the internet. Hours on social media, clicking links, flicking through apps. Sucked down the rabbit hole of nothingness. Hours of my life just thrown in the bin. Gone. Like precious dollar bills fed into a slot machine that win you nothing. I'd gambled away so much time on something that gave nothing back, and that was a painful truth.

We're so afraid of being bored; we're practically programmed to fear it and avoid it at all costs. A powerfully charged distraction fell right into our laps. Twitter feeds. Instagram posts. Always updating, always flickering, always pulling us away from where we were into something and somewhere else. Into the void. Social media had given me a place to share and to discover, but just like the tiresome ritual of photographing everything I ate, it had become mere habit, a time-suck, and it wasn't a valuable exchange. In the end I wore my smartphone like a boredom prosthetic and used the internet as a stop-gap for thought. Digital Polyfilla in the spaces where ideas might have bloomed. Day after day I was hungrily digesting information I didn't even care about, barely retained and sure as hell didn't need. Jesus, when I think of all the things I might have done with that time...the books I might have read, the skills I might have picked up, the things I might have achieved. The things I might have written! Had I just given my mind the chance to be bored, and present. To offer it space to wander free and aimlessly instead of jamming it full of other people's projections and trivial stimuli. All that time-wasting was just that; it had given me nothing back but had taken so much opportunity away. I'd wasted so much time. So much life.

I did not regret the person I was. If I regretted anything else, it was not *accepting* who I was, not embracing her fully, and wasting so much of what I was capable of on the fear of not getting it right. Of being vulnerable.

If we're going to get right down to it, my greatest regret was fear. The utter, bloody pointlessness of it.

That was the regret. Wasting all that precious time distracting myself from putting myself out there, connecting, creating, finding my voice. Precious time frittered away. And on what, I can't even recall.

All day the sun had been gradually creeping its way closer to the thumb-shaped overhang until it eventually slipped behind it, liberating my face from the burning-hot glare I'd been suffering all day and stretching long, late-afternoon shadows across the clearing. I felt the relief of having the sun move off the upper half of my body but also a sudden churn of dread that came with the closing of the day. The sudden release from the heat mixed with intense fear sent another wave of chills through me, my teeth chattering and body quaking.

I do not want to spend the night out here.

At no point had I thought I would be out here at night, let alone by myself. And now the evening was sinking in over the desert. Nightfall would change the status of my predicament from serious to severe. I was facing what I knew would be the longest night of my life. All I could do was lie there and wait for darkness to fall.

Brace yourself.

As the dark set in so did the cold, settling over my body like a damp shroud. It's amazing how quickly the temperature can slide. Wearing only my vest and my denim shorts, my limbs were exposed to the plummeting cool of the night. My T-shirt was the only extra layer I had and I pulled it over my head, grateful that it was a size too big and therefore loose enough to make it possible for me to gently, gently, tug it down and around my torso.

What else could I work with?

There was a plastic grocery bag in my rucksack which had contained my lunchbox and the CamelBak – this could be useful. I upended the contents of the bag and considered how I might use it for warmth. My first thought was that I could fashion it into a pair of trousers for my lower legs; if I could make two holes in the end maybe I could pull it over my feet and my shins. I started to tear a hole in each bottom corner, using my teeth and my fingers to stretch the thick, white plastic until I had spaces where my feet might fit through. A plastic pair of shorts.

But how the hell was I going to get that over my legs? Not only were my boots too big and chunky to get through the holes, but there was no way I could reach them. I hooked the bag over the stick and tried to manoeuvre the open end over my right foot. My boot was still far too big for the hole I'd made, so I hoisted the bag back up to my chest and went about tearing at the holes to expand them. I tried again to hook the bag over my boot but still I couldn't get it through. It was tedious work; with gritted teeth and neck straining I swore at the thing.

Fucking go through, you fucking fucker!

But I couldn't do it. Despondency. Frustration. The creeping cold. Instead I tore the whole end of the bag open, turning it into a kind of plastic tube skirt that I could hopefully get over both feet at once. But I still didn't have the reach or momentum needed to hook the bag over my boots, yank it under their immovable dead weight, and then pull it up towards me.

This was not going to work.

In the end I simply draped the tattered bag over my legs, another layer in addition to the map that was already covering them. I wrapped the bandana around my throat and tucked it into the neck of my t-shirt. I pulled the rucksack over one arm like a sleeve; the inside of the blue canvas was plasticky and cold against my bare skin but still far better than the chill of the outside air. My other arm I retracted inside the t-shirt sleeve, letting it rest on my belly, and tucked the sleeve inside itself to keep out the chill. As long as I could keep night the air off me, I should be all right.

While I felt somewhat protected from the chill, I was still so terribly, terribly cold. And I sure as hell didn't feel protected from anything else. As I lay there watching the sky grow from a deep navy blue to absolute black, all I could think about was snakes.

I know that snakes aren't nocturnal. I know they don't usually come out at night, when it's colder. But then I don't usually sleep on the floor of the desert.

We all get scared of things, no matter whether it's rational or reasonable or whether there is any chance in hell that the thing we fear will ever show up. We are afraid of spiders even if they won't hurt us, just because they're spiders. In the dark, we get spooked by thoughts of ghosts despite not being sure they exist. Those childhood monsters, that crocodile under the bed, only seemed to be a concern once the light was turned out. Being alone in the dark is when our minds let our fears run wild and free. It's why, even as an adult, hearing strange noises when you're alone in your house can make you so unnerved you feel compelled to sleep with the lights on. You know you'll feel foolish in the daylight but right now, it's dark. The dark is when the things we avoid come out.

Darkness is the stomping ground for fear.

And where I was currently lying, it had now become very dark indeed.

On my hikes I'd had one eye on the lookout for snakes. There was a part of me that wanted to see one because we don't get snakes in New Zealand and the idea of spotting one in the wild was thrilling. That is, as long as I did not step on one. This was slap bang in the first half of rattlesnake season, and I'd been doing some reading on where they hang out, what to do if you see one and, most importantly, what to do if you get bitten by one.

Stay still.

Don't run.

Keep the bitten extremity elevated.

Don't try to suck out the venom.

Don't use a tourniquet.

Don't lance the bite or apply ice or heat.

Remove any rings or watches in case of swelling.

Serious symptoms can occur within minutes...so get to a hospital as fast as you can.

Rattlesnake bites in Joshua Tree are frequent enough – in southern California about 200 people on average get bitten every year. I couldn't stop thinking about it.

'Do you know how much a vial of antivenom is?' I'd told Nat and Lou, citing an article I'd read. '*Two thousand dollars.* And if you get bitten you'd need six to eight of them. *Six to eight.*'

I'd become a little obsessed by the risk, so much so that I had explicitly taken out travel insurance with unlimited medical coverage in case of a bite. That had been the biggest concern on my mind, coming into the desert: being bitten by a rattlesnake.

Now here I was, with a smashed pelvis, in a hole in the middle of the desert, immobile on the ground – at snake level – in the deep dark of night. It didn't matter what the common fucking habitual behaviour of snakes was at this point. I was scared out of my mind.

The darkness of the desert is thick and yawning, being so far from the tremendous light pollution of civilisation. I am not afraid of the dark, but in this situation I found myself in, I was terrified of what might be in it.

Fear does crazy things to a person, I guess, because I became convinced that I could see snakes. They were everywhere. I squinted into the darkness at a long shape on a nearby boulder and realized that it was very, very slowly moving across the rock. I froze, terrified, but as the minutes ticked by, I realized that, despite its undulating slither, it wasn't inching forward. Slowly, I moved my trembling hands to my phone, I switched on the torch function and pointed the beam of light at the snake on the rock.

There was nothing there.

I was baffled, unsure how I could see something so clearly and yet for it to have never existed. Then I heard the tiniest crackle of a twig and saw a movement to my right on the ground, emerging from the deep blackness of the gap below the overhanging rock. A snake appeared, sticking out its long head, moving slowly towards me. Or…was it moving? Again, I stared hard into the darkness at it, willing it to retreat. When it didn't seem to be getting any closer, I switched on the phone torch…

There was nothing there.

This went on for much of the night. I didn't get much sleep.

Day Two: Wednesday

I must have fallen asleep eventually because, at some point, I woke up.

A sound had woken me. A rattling.

My eyelids prised open and took in the pale jigsaw of grey sky cut out by the boulders looming above me. My body was stiff and sore, the weight of the solid earth pressing into my heels and back and buttocks.

So it really happened.

This hadn't been one of those nightmares, the really vivid ones in which you're falling, hurtling down, then you jolt awake before you hit the ground.

That had been real.

What about the rattling?

What was that?

Dazed by exhaustion I listened intently, trying to figure out what the sound was and where it was coming from.

It took a moment to realize it was coming from me.

It was my teeth, chattering uncontrollably. A night spent exposed to the chill, even with my best efforts to stay warm, had pushed my body to the edge. My system, I guess, had gone into shock. I took deep, dry breaths, trying to slow my clattering teeth and calm my heart to a regular beat. And in a few minutes the rattling stopped. I rubbed my arms, longing for warmth to come, and at the same time I dreaded it.

It was not quite sunrise; the distant sky to my left was becoming lighter, but the clearing was still enveloped in the cold, dark greyness of shadow; even the highest boulders above me were yet to be swept in sunlight. Based on the palette of the sky – grey-blue and still speckled with the last faded stars – I could guess the time;

I recalled how it had looked just the previous morning when I'd got up and made coffee. It must only be about 5.30am. I checked my iPhone – I was bang on. But it would be at least four hours until the sun reached me. My body tensed against the chill, as if my skin was trying to huddle in on itself.

You know how it is when you're uncomfortably hot – say, a sticky summer's day in the heat of the city – and all you long for is shade. Or a pool. Or some serious air conditioning. And when you are freezing cold you long for warmth in any which way it comes. Enduring either discomfort, it's hard to imagine ever wanting it. Yesterday I had longed for the relief of coolness and now, in the chill of the early morning, I ached for sunlight to warm my skin.

I daydreamed of being in a warm bed. The firm nestle of a mattress. Soft sheets. The weight of a thick winter-season duvet. Better than that, the electric blanket that made those icy London winters so delicious. When I would slip under my thick, white bedding into radiating warmth, so that without intending to I'd let out a blissful *aaahhhhh* every time.

A small sip of water from the CamelBak soothed my throat, which was dry and scratchy. The cold air seemed to have sucked me of moisture and I swaddled my cracked lips in a thick layer of lip balm.

I noticed the urine I'd collected in my bottle overnight looked dark, almost orange. Not a familiar colour. Did this mean there was blood in it? I wondered again if I had damaged something internally. I was in enough pain that it would be hard to know.

Adding insult to injury, I'm a life-long side sleeper and the urge to roll onto my side was overwhelming. I had now been lying flat on my back for hours, stuck in the same position. When you sit down for a long time – say, in a theatre, through a drawn-out performance with no interval, you'll start to shuffle around or simply have to get up and move about, maybe even rub your backside until the discomfort subsides. That's how I felt, except it was my whole body, in agony with the extended pressure against the hard ground. I couldn't get up and move about. I couldn't so much as shuffle. Everything pressed into the earth, aching and groaning.

God, I longed to roll over.

I stared up at the ghost of the moon, still hanging around in the pale blanket of the sky. There was nothing blissful about my bed here on the hard, rocky dirt. But I had survived the night. And that meant the worst was over. If I could get through that, I could get through the rest of this day. Because with the morning came hope, a renewed sense of optimism and a growing excitement in having a whole new day ahead, a whole day for someone to come and find me.

And once they did, I would be OK.

[video] *Well, I survived the night. It was very, very cold and very, very long and very, very uncomfortable. Um, and there's blood in my urine so I am beginning to worry if I don't get someone to come and rescue me today I'm in big trouble. But, you know, it's about 5.30 in the morning – sunrise. So hopefully today someone will hear me shouting and I can get to a hospital. So fingers crossed. My legs work...Just my pelvis doesn't. So...could be worse, I suppose? I've decided I'm going to survive this. Because this is not how my story ends. It would be kind of a bummer...I've got a bagel and I have enough water to last me for a little while. So, I'm just going*

to keep shouting. And I hope maybe Nat and Lou, who know that I've come on this trek, suspect something when they don't get any response from me and maybe figure out that I've got into trouble. It's really...my only chance of getting out of here. But I'm going to survive it, I just really hope I don't have to spend another night in here. I really hope I don't. So. Fingers crossed.

Speaking into the camera gave me something to do, as if sharing what I was going through meant that, for that one brief moment, I wasn't alone. There was comfort in it. Experiencing this alone was too hard. This black box of plastic was as much a companion as I could conjure up here in this desolate, hopeless place.

Then something flew towards me at a terrifying speed.

Small, dark and buzzing, it zipped down from the overhanging rocks, then paused abruptly about an arm's length from my face. It was a hummingbird, hovering a few inches from my nose for just a fleeting second. The sound of it was like a tiny radio-controlled plane, and immediately my hand moved up in front of my face with the fright of it. The bird zipped away. The whole visit was over in seconds. My heart was racing from the surprise and the speed of it. But I really hoped it would come back. A hummingbird is a harmless, beautiful thing and in the realm of desert creatures, this one was friendly. I needed friendly.

The desert life was sussing me out. I wondered what else might appear today. Might I get a visit from a coyote? Might the snakes come out with the sun, now that my initial crash and shuffles were finished? My lack of movement could work against me. I just hoped if anything came by it would be human. Someone.

Anyone.

LONDON

People could fuck the fuck off.
   Seriously.
   Some tall bloke in a suit had just knocked my bag, jostling it as it hung from my shoulder, thereby jostling me, and I was *furious*. The Tube platform was crowded, like it always was at this time of the morning, but it wasn't *that* crowded. Not so packed that he had to bang into my bag. I looked down the platform: he had so much space to walk down, a good two or three metres in which to swing his weight but no, he had to come right up to the edge and get in my personal space. Look at him, marching on, no awareness. *Fuckwit.*
   I wasn't always this cantankerous. Was I? When had that changed; when had I become this person – angry, impatient, irritable? For much of my life I had considered myself a genuinely positive person. An eternal optimist. When I first joined Twitter that had actually been my bio line, 'Eternal optimist'. That's how strongly I felt it defined me. Now I didn't feel like that at all. Who the hell was that version of me? I no longer had a definition for who I was becoming.
   And *why* was I so pissed off?
   It was easy enough to blame the commute. The Tube was always too busy, too pushy, and everybody was so aggressive. Of course I would get cranky. Everyone was cranky. Except it wasn't the commute. Not really. It was something so much deeper than that.

Peering sideways, I watched the other commuters lining up along the platform edge, men dressed in shirts and ties, women freshly accessorised for the day ahead, labourers in grubby hoodies and hi-vis vests – people coming from different places, going to different places, but all of them here, crossing over in this one intersection of time and space. Almost all of them staring at their phones, oblivious to life around them. Everyone withdrawn into their own shell. Shutting out the rest of the world.

I understood that. This is how we survive in a place like London. There were more than nine million of us sharing this little cross-hatch of concrete and each of us had formed a protective bubble, a tiny scrap of safe space to retreat into.

Which is why, when the man in the suit crashed into my bag, I felt rage, saw the red mist descend, felt my veins vibrating with irritation. I was ready to snap.

I felt like this a lot these days.

Just the previous day I'd been wading through that familiar black malaise. Sunday-morning blues. I must have paced the flat for a good hour before I conjured up the courage to go out.

At first, when I woke, I mistook it for tiredness, a weight that pressed into me, dissolving any hope of motivation. But once I got up, I realized everything was not OK. I was not OK. And it wasn't so much that I felt down, rather, I kind of felt...nothing.

Numb. This was new. And it was too soon to decide whether the numbness was worse than the anger. Neither were conducive to my going outside.

What was the point in going anywhere?

But I needed to get out from inside these walls. I'd spent Friday night and all day Saturday at home, eschewing any guilt about my voluntary confinement by promising myself I'd go out on Sunday. When I got into these moods I withdrew into myself, and the greatest danger was going from Friday night to Monday morning not only without talking to anyone, but without actually leaving the flat. Mara didn't live here any more – like so many others, she'd moved away. She'd chased her dream to make wine in northern California.

And what was I doing? Nothing.

That had to change. I would force myself out. I *wanted* to go out. Autumn was my favourite season, London in the midst of golden splendour, when the good people of the city make their way to Hampstead Heath. I longed to do the same, joining the seasonal pilgrims for a walk on the heath, then maybe go sit in a cafe for a bit.

But the idea of actually going outside felt too big, too overwhelming, as if heading into the world without purpose might actually shatter me somehow.

Staying in felt unbearable and going out seemed impossible. I was torn between the two.

I distracted myself. Flipped the mattress. Made my bed. Then I put my face into it and screamed – a long, muffled howl. I did not understand what I was feeling and all I wanted was for someone to put their arms around me and tell me everything was going to be all right. But I couldn't think of a single person who would do that and say that and have me truly believe them. I sat on the edge of the bed, clutching a pillow against my stomach, and tried to feel excited about something. Anything. But I couldn't. I was numb. *Isn't this what depression is supposed to feel like?* I heard the question in my head and immediately dismissed it.

This isn't depression. I'm not depressed. That's not me, not who I am.
I was still functioning, wasn't I?
Look, would a depressed person go out? Like this?
I grabbed my coat and pulled the door closed behind me, feeling the bite of autumn air on my face and thinking I might come to feel better after all, just by being outside. I took the Tube to Hampstead, strolled along the cobbles of Flask Walk, stopping briefly to look at the antiques and trinkets piled outside a little shop. I'd flicked through a box of tattered records, something I can never resist, but I wasn't paying any attention to the names on the sleeves. My heart wasn't in it; it was all for show. I was playing at feeling normal.

Shoving my hands into the pocket of my coat, I carried on towards the heath, through the picture-postcard streets of huge old houses and Victorian-esque street lamps, the narrow roads hemmed in by big red-brick walls and overhanging trees, until I was consumed by the calming shades of yellow of the park. The splendour of it took my breath away...Yet I still felt numb. How strange, to acknowledge something but not be able to feel it. The main avenue was embraced by the tall arms of trees and along it there were people out walking their dogs, walking with the sole purpose of simply being there on the heath. To be among autumn. Just like me. There was some comfort to belonging.

Maybe I'd go to a cafe and write? I'd been suffering pains in my wrists for so many months that writing had become difficult, but I had so much noise in my head that it would help to get it down on paper. As it was Sunday all of the cafes near the park were teeming with people, perched in windows or huddled on spindly-legged tables in the street. Affectionate couples in snuggly knitwear with their dogs, families with buggies, people devouring the papers along with their toast and eggs. I stood on the opposite side of the street, unable to bring myself to cross. I was on another island entirely.

Why do I feel like this? Why can't I be one of the happy people?

My doctor had told me I was depressed. But was I? Perhaps it was more a case that I was not being completely true to myself any more. I was half a person, living a half-life. It was a perfectly *nice* life, don't get me wrong...but you can't live half a nice life to the full.

I thought of Mara, amongst the vines in the northern California sun. I remember the day she left, watching her get into a taxi to the airport with her suitcase and hat, off to change the course of her life. I remember how empty the flat had suddenly felt, but how much admiration I had felt for her then, in recognizing she needed to go in a completely different direction. I needed to do the same for myself. I honestly no longer knew where I was going.

Even now. All I could bring myself to do was walk.

I'd wandered away from the yellows of the heath and now found myself in the grey of the residential streets, the sky a sheet of concrete. After an hour or so, I was feeling the cold and starting to get thirsty. Perhaps it was time I went home. But I couldn't face being holed up in the flat again. Not yet. The thought of going back there made it hard to breathe, as if the walls had already toppled inwards and were crushing me.

A bus had pulled up. And I got on it, not knowing or caring where it was going. Glued to my seat, my forehead pressed against the filthy glass as we passed through the centre of London with its throngs of shoppers and tourists, I didn't move until it eventually terminated outside Hyde Park.

The park was lit up entirely in the colours of the season, paths cut neatly through a sea of vivid yellows and I took one heading south, skirting around the duck lake. I recognized places from years ago; memories were planted everywhere here, as abundant as the trees. In my twenties I would come to this park whenever I felt lost or alone, or when I simply wanted to enjoy a little space in the vibrating heart of London. The day I landed in London with my big, blue, secondhand backpack, knowing no one, having no plan other than to make one, I had found my way to this park and sat under a tree. Taking it all in. Feeling like it might be the only place I could gather my thoughts. To see it all lit up in gold like this, I wanted to burst into tears.

I was a dam, close to cracking, waiting to crumble.

Not here. Not now.

I'm really not OK.

But I held it in. And somehow, I swallowed it down.

The screech of the incoming train drew the commuters on the platform into a huddle, closing in on the platform edge. I moved forward too and closed my eyes. I liked to do this sometimes, stand right on the yellow line and feel the full weight of the train slam the air, racing past me just an arm's length from my nose.

It was a way to shake me out of my fugue, slapping me into sensibility, reminding me I'm alive.

The doors of the train carriage opened and everybody pushed

and twisted and shunted as one into what little space there was inside. I joined the writhing sea of armpits as hands reached for poles and handles. Seated passengers tucked their limbs in, wrapping arms around bags, coats around chests. Every head remained lowered to stare at phone screens. We were all zombies, here, weren't we? Existing. Autopilot. Going through the motions. Day in, day out. As a species we learn to adapt to the world around us. With so many of us jostling for space every day, we were all falling into the same step. We are products of our environment, I thought to myself, and took some deep breaths, trying to shake off the buzzing of irritation that still hummed through my veins.

It was only 8.15am. I still had a lot of day to get through. A lot of cantankering to do.

My commute spat me out at Oxford Circus station, leaving me to the bit of my journey I actually rather enjoyed, the walk through Soho. To me it felt like a village. A busy, dirty village, but one of cobbled streets and shutters, the faint fragrance of stale beer and fresh coffee mingling with the occasional cloying stench from a doorway. Like so much of London it was grubby but somehow still romantic in a way that few things can be.

The monochrome mock-Tudor facade of Liberty's department store loomed ahead as I marched toward Carnaby Street, into its avenue of bright signage, pretending as I so often did that I was on the set of a film of some sort. A small moment of escapism. I crossed the busy cobbles of the streets, skipping quickly between the aggressive approach of black cabs and delivery vans, passing the *Big Issue* seller in his red vest chirping his sing-song 'Good morning, *Big Issue*' to everyone who hurried by, ignoring him. I ignored him too, as I always did, making a wan smile but not looking him in the eye, instead slipping through the glass revolving doors of my office building and into obscurity, just like everybody else.

———

I was a sub-editor on a major food magazine, making me a pedant and a glutton, and I loved it. My desk, on the long double row that housed the whole team, was always piled high with draft pages, cookbooks and the detritus of foodstuffs sent in from PRs and marketeers. There was always food around in the office. It was an occupational hazard for which nobody had fully developed enough self-restraint. Wherever you looked there were half-devoured packets of things – fancy biscuits, gourmet crisps, exotic produce, curious looking jars and bottles, not to mention a wicker basket full of discarded weird ingredients that nobody wanted but which none of us could bring ourselves to simply throw out. The results of recipe testing meant my freezer was often stuffed with the sorts of things that made no sense out of context – after late-night drinks I could easily come home to an empty pantry and wind up defrosting a slab of venison pie, eating it in my pyjamas and wondering who the hell I was.

Nights out were spent at restaurants, bars, pop-ups and launches, surrounded by other foodies – it was a term that seemed to leave a sour taste in one's mouth, but for desperate want of a better word that's what we were. Food writers, bloggers, magazine staffers, restaurant PRs and hangers-on, gathering to taste and sample, to see and be seen, and all the while photographing every meal, every cocktail, every cup of coffee. Above restaurant tables a sea of smartphones, angled this way and that as the beholders crouched and stretched, all trying to capture the best shot. It was behaviour so habitual, and very easily justifiable as part of one's job, whether it was work-related or not. Somewhere in the midst of it, the lines between work and play became blurred, like a buttery fingerprint on an iPhone lens.

'If you didn't post it on Instagram did you even really eat it?' We all knew the joke, but we were in it together. A community. Of people who were embarrassing to dine out with.

I was one of them. And I was a part of something.

The mag team was a dysfunctional family of seven, having been through the wringer of the changing publishing industry and widespread problems, tightened belts and acquisitions. What was left was barely holding it together: sliced budgets; cheapened paper stock; a magazine clinging on for dear life. And, as such, our already diminishing team felt like we were pushed to the edge, barely hanging on by our fingertips. Over the years we'd relocated and shrunk, our office now a small corner on a big floor of weekly magazines, tucked away beside the IT department. But we kept on keeping on. We clung on out of what can only be described as love. We had given this publication so much of ourselves, and we refused to let it go.

Despite the stress and publishing politics, what I liked so much about my job was the comforting familiarity of it. We were a team who had, for the most part, been working together for years, a collaboration of vastly different temperaments and talents. Seated at our length of desk like a gathering of relatives round the table for the holidays, there were moods, disagreements and irritations (not to mention too much food), but with it all an affection that, for me, made coming into the office feel a bit like coming home.

I had a place here. It was an anchor, keeping my feet on the ground. Although sometimes I wondered how I got here. And all too often I sensed I was afraid that if this was cut loose I would float away entirely.

All my life I had worked to build a life just like the one I was living...

Now that I had it, I didn't actually know what I was supposed to do with it.

It didn't help that I felt like I was winging it. Rather than owning my place as an experienced woman in media who deserved to be there, I felt riddled with self-doubt, as if I was actually two Labradors in a trenchcoat and sooner or later everyone would realize. Underneath my skin I was building up a fireball of anxiety that only grew in ferocity the more successful my outer life became – or at least, appeared to be. To the outside observer, my life in London would have looked pretty fantastic. Yet I felt lost. It was almost as if the better my life looked on paper, the more hollow I felt underneath. How did I not see that paper is too flimsy to build a life on?

Then there was the chaser: the guilt. That visceral, heartburn of awful guilt of not being happy, which merely piled on to my unhappiness, stacked higher and higher, like overdue filing. I believed I was successful, ergo, I should be happy! So why wasn't I?

I could feel this anxiety getting worse over time, manifesting itself in bad habits, in the sort of men I pursued – the kind who expected nothing of me but only left me feeling more empty, the less seen I felt. The habitual social drinking, followed by the inevitable self-loathing, of trying to cut back but failing the temptation of industry soirées and booze-laden events. Of trying to stay fit and look after myself while most of the time just being too exhausted. There were the many months of insomnia. And then came the slew of random pains in my body.

First my right wrist began playing up: a burning feeling in the thumb joint, which I stubbornly ignored. I put it down to overuse, changed to a more ergonomic keyboard and ploughed on. *It'll go away.* Except it didn't. It spread to the rest of my hand and fingers. It became too painful to wear my watch, or anything on my arms – except for the plastic moulded cast provided by a physiotherapist. Typing and wielding a pen, both the tools of my trade, became increasingly difficult but all I could do was push on with it.

Within a year, my left wrist started to feel the same burning and the months passed in an exhausting blur of attempts to manage whatever the hell this was. Desk assessments, dictation apps on my phone, an ongoing chain of specialist appointments. Eventually I gave up cycling, gym classes, yoga. And, perhaps because of all this, a few months later my back started playing up, too. A weekly physiotherapist appointment was added to my calendar. I wasn't sure which was more excruciating – the pain itself or feeling like an invalid. I felt weak.

I hated feeling weak.

It was the same reason why I kept my creeping anxiety to myself as much as I could, swallowing it down, as if keeping it buried would make me stronger.

Instead, I was beginning to crack.

Time is an abstract concept. I'd been spouting that line since high school. I didn't know whether I'd heard it somewhere or made it up but I still used it now, usually when I was trying to be funny.

But time had never been as difficult – or felt as abstract – as it was out here. Keeping track of it wasn't easy... For the moment, at least, I had my iPhone, which could give me nothing in terms of communication with anyone, but it gave me a working clock. I checked in now and then, measuring how accurate my own gauge of time was, and occasionally throwing desperate, hopeful glances at the signal.

And then, at 8.51am, the screen went black.

Fuck.

I knew the phone was running low on battery and that this was bound to happen soon enough, but when it actually went flat I felt surprised somehow. A cold rush of fear in my veins. It didn't matter that I hadn't been able to get any signal on it...just having it still felt like hope. The phone was my one and only means of communication, working or not, and there was still a part of me that believed a signal might still get through. Somehow. Or, that if someone was looking for me, they might be able to track my location. There was technology for that, I knew that much; technology that could ping my phone and figure out where I was. I needed this phone. Having it on had offered some peace of mind. As time kept on creeping forward, my little lifelines were falling by the wayside. And the unstoppable reality of this was terrifying. I could do nothing but watch them disappear one by one.

I had no idea how fruitful it was to scream for help, I just did

it anyway. It was a task best saved for the morning hours, before
the sun hit, as the expelling of air from my lungs would make my
head spin and leave my mouth and throat sore and dry. Although
sometimes I just had to scream anyway, release the driving
desperation and fear that pounded through my body. Alternating
between a drawn out cry of *HELP ME!* and *SOMEBODY HELP
ME PLEASE!*, mixing up the vowel sounds and emphasis both
for my personal sanity and in case one or the other was better
at carrying distances. I'd scream like this for a good ten minutes
or so at a time, then have a rest, and take a sip of water from the
CamelBak. Tiny sips, although I longed to gulp mouthfuls. I was
all too aware that I had to make this water last. I just didn't know
how long for.

As soon as the sun crept over my body again, that fear in my
veins went from cold to hot with it, morphing into anger and
frustration.

*What the fuck am I going to do now? How am I going to get out of
here? I don't have a phone any more. What the hell am I going to do
about it?*

It was extraordinarily infuriating that here I was, conscious,
coherent and with full potential to recover from my injuries if
I got medical help right now...But I just couldn't move. That
single factor was my death knell. How agonizing, to be lying here,
helpless, unable to do anything! I had always been able to take care
of myself. It was just the way I was, the way I'd always done things;
and now, when I really, really needed to help myself, I couldn't.

Could I?

I twisted my head towards the gap the rocks on my left. I
couldn't get up...but what if I could still get *out*? What if I

could somehow roll myself onto my front and use my arms to drag myself out? Crawling on my belly like one of those devout religious pilgrims, could I find my way to freedom? At least get closer to the trail?

This was an impossible, ludicrous idea. The pain was unendurable and my bones too broken; my body was as good as glued to the ground. I couldn't so much as raise myself onto my elbows...But *I was fired up*. I would get myself out of this place! Fuck this situation! I was prepared to try anything! For all of the pain in the world, it had to be better than dying, right? What did I have to lose?

Everything, if I didn't try.

Since my body couldn't move itself I would have to find a way to do it manually. This would require some engineering. I came up with a plan to lever myself up, and I jammed the end of the hiking stick under my right hip, wincing as I twisted it in tight, trying to get it as far underneath me as I could while gaining some traction in the dirt...essentially, I was setting up a makeshift car jack. Slowly, slowly, with all the adrenaline-frenzied delicacy of a movie hero defusing a bomb, I lifted the stick towards my body, raising my right hip from the ground about a quarter of an inch. I grimaced, gritting my teeth hard as pain shot through me.

Breathe.

I lifted it again. Another quarter inch.

More pain.

Ahhhhhhhh!

Breathe.

Pain or death. Pain or death.

The blue wire or the red wire.

Breathe.

Another lift.

Another quarter inch.

Time rolled by; I don't know how long. But I continued this pace, moving precariously slowly, feeling pain as far as I could take it without triggering that ultimate agony of dislodging my pelvic bones, taking every twitch and nudge carefully – so, so carefully. After some time, my teeth still clenched hard, I had got my right hip what felt like it must have been a good three inches off the ground – a guess, of course, as I couldn't see. But it felt like progress, and something akin to optimism was creeping in a little. My head pounded with the concentration, breath held with the determination.

Come on, Claire, you're doing it. You're really doing it.

You're going to roll over. You're going to get yourself out of here.

And then it happened.

The bomb went off.

My pelvis made a crunching, grinding sound as it collapsed on itself.

Crunch-crunch-crunch-crunch-click-click-click.

A horrifying scream.

I felt my bladder let go.

And then a second, frozen in that agonizing position, wanting to drop the stick immediately and fall back to the ground but knowing I'd have to go through the same burst of pain in order to lower myself again, as the shards of bones crunched back into place.

I had no choice.

Down I went.

Another animal scream, the echo falling away in seconds.

My head was spinning with pain, dizzy, swimming violently, and I thought I might be sick, if only I had anything to throw up.

And after all of that, I was on my back again.

Back to square one.

As the aftershocks of the pain shivered through my body I took slow breaths, trying to slow my racing heart and gather myself.

No. No way. I cannot try that again.

I can't.

I yanked the stick out from under me and slumped it on the ground next to me, panting, my arms splayed on the dirt, hands shaking.

Fuck.

I'm not actually sure this pain is better than death.

From where I was lying, the result was going to be the same either way.

If I passed out in this heat I felt there was the very real risk I might not regain consciousness. Or I might not regain consciousness quickly enough to rehydrate. Who knows. All I knew was that I was running out of options.

I'd been lying there a short while, breathing heavily as the waves of pain slowly eased, when a movement by the rocks to my right caught my eye. I felt my whole body tense up. I'd been constantly monitoring this rock out of the corner of my eye as the dark gaping hollow beneath it seemed a terribly inviting hideout for a snake. And now something was there. I slowly turned my head to look, but instead of a predator beneath the rock there appeared a lizard atop it. It was about six inches from head to tail, out to bask in the heat, and he stood squat and sturdy, head high, surveying his kingdom.

I smiled. 'Hi,' I breathed, not wanting to scare him off. We stayed there like that for some time...both of us completely still, not so much as a twitch giving the lizard away, as I took in his grey-green body, and regal stance.

I like lizards. As kids we were always looking for them. There was a section of fence that ran along the outside of the dunes near the school recreation centre that was such a prime spot for sunbathing skinks that my brothers and friends and I called it 'the lizard farm'. We'd go down there just to catch them, armed with Mum's best plastic containers, which would become temporary housing for the poor skinks we'd snatch from the fence. We'd take them home to observe and prod, to pick up – gently, thumb and forefinger under the forearms, never by the tail. That was something you learned young, that a lizard can drop its tail to escape. Not that they'd get far; often they'd race under the bureau, where one or more of the family cats would sit in wait for them.

I gazed at the lizard sunning himself in front of me.

I guess the tables have turned now, eh, mate?

And then, completely unexpectedly, the lizard began doing push-ups.

Up–down–up–down–up–down.

I'd never seen a lizard do this and it was so unexpected and funny, I couldn't help myself – I chuckled. It came out as rumble in my throat, then a squeak, the noise sending the lizard darting back into the crevice of the rock.

'Come back, little guy!' I rasped, gazing longingly at the space he had occupied. I was doing a great job of deterring anything that came close, even though I wanted the company.

Typical of you.

I'd thought I'd known what loneliness was. Before. Out here in the desert, this was something else. Not only was I so physically isolated from everyone – not just everyone I knew...literally everyone – but nobody had even noticed I was missing. This was the position I had put myself in, in every sense. And it really would be the death of me.

I wished I could drop my tail and run.

———————————————

The hat wasn't cutting it. Despite all my best efforts to hold it up on the end of the hiking stick, it hung there limply, not blocking out enough of the sun, which I still felt creeping on to my arms and torso. My arms wobbled wearily as I took turns alternating from one to another. It was hard work.

The idea came to me that I could create some kind of curtain, something wider, to keep more of the sun off me. I had tried using physio tape to hang the battered and torn map over the end of the stick, but it had only drooped pathetically, a flag without a breeze, and proved even less helpful than my hat. I took down the crumpled paper and felt the weight of the sun bear down on me, the familiar and unbearable burn spurring me on in my project.

I would need to get creative with what I had. Improvise. 'Kiwi ingenuity' they called that back home.

Turning my head and scanning the clearing, I spotted a thin but reasonably sturdy-looking stick, about the length of my arm, a couple of metres away and used my hiking stick to drag it towards me. I yanked out the hair tie from my ponytail and used it to bind both sticks together in a 't' shape. Then, to really secure the frame, I tore off a strip of the physio tape in my first aid kit and wrapped that around the binding. Satisfied, I looked up at my creation.

Oh my god.

I was holding a crucifix.

Christ almighty.

Imagine me dying and someone finding that.

The next step was to make something to go over it. I tore my tattered grocery bag right down one side seam, making a long, raggedy rectangle of plastic and stretched this from one side of the cross to the other, piercing it on each end of the branch. Finally, I placed my hat on the top, like a jaunty Christmas-tree angel. Now I had a decent sunshield to work with. While it still took effort to hold the stick upright for hours on end, I didn't have to raise my arms. I stared up at the grocery bag. It was from Stater Bros grocery, a few days ago, when I'd picked up a few things for the hike, and for the barbecue at Jo and Jef's. Who would've thought this is what it would next get used for?

Jo and Jef were the other friends I'd met through Nat and Lou. Jo was a writer and editor from Australia, Jef a comic illustrator from Long Beach, and I'd warmed to them immediately – the sort of easy-going, generous folks you meet and instantly want to spend more time with. *Good eggs*, as we say back home. The fact I was in their house, joining them and their out of town friends for a barbecue was a case in point: they'd known I was on my own and invited me for dinner.

Jef waggled one of the little vintage glasses he'd recently picked up for Jo at a swap meet.

'Desert martini?'

Homemade gin – cheap grocery store vodka infused with juniper berries that were picked from out in the desert. Although I was trying to cut back on the drink – for the sake of my head and also because I was feeling overly cautious about driving home in Lou's car – I couldn't turn down a chance to drink a cocktail like that.

'Ahhhh, go on then.'

Jef gave me a nod that said I'd made the right decision and went about mixing martinis. I noticed his white T-shirt had the word SPAGHETTI written on it in Sharpie. The first, and previous time we'd met, he wore a T-shirt on which he had simply written ENYA, for reasons unknown to me.

They had friends visiting from San Francisco. 'The spare room is taken but you're welcome to the couch if you want to stay over,' said Jo. We took our cocktails to the gathering in the living room, where I perched myself on the floor. I was surprised how easy it was to slip into the circle, warming quickly to this wonderful bunch of eclectic, creative and interesting humans. There were no airs or graces, no reflex to hide parts of myself, just easy openness. That seemed to be the way out here. Jo told me how she'd stumbled upon Natalie's Instagram profile and felt, as a fellow Australian implanted in Joshua Tree, the urge to reach out.

'I'm not normally one to message a stranger like that,' she said. 'But I figured, what the hell, it's not easy meeting new people out here, so fuck it. And now...I'm glad I went out of my comfort zone.' We clinked our glasses, all around the circle.

That's the thing about connections. Everybody is a link in a chain. Open yourself to one connection and the opportunity for others will follow. I'd forgotten how valuable that is.

It was a chain I now found myself warmly and suddenly clasped to the end of.

After dinner, once bellies were full and plates cleared, we stayed sitting round the table, telling tales of antics amid so much laughter I thought my ribs would bruise. It felt so easy; I was a stranger, but one invited in with open arms. This is connection. This is how it works. I went home happy.

It was a sensation I felt so keenly that the next night I shared those sentiments in an email to my mum. We communicated through sporadic email updates, the time difference between New Zealand and wherever I was always creating confusion to Skype calls, which had to be planned in advance.

I'm halfway through my time in Joshua Tree...I will be very sad to leave. There's a really wonderful sense of community here; not necessarily wholesome, but in a way which allows people to be unapologetically themselves and nobody judges. Lou left me his Mini Cooper to drive so as to save on a rental car, and although it's a manual I've got the hang of it now. I love throwing on my old shorts, a singlet and a hat, chucking my hiking boots in the back and driving down the long, straight roads to find hiking trails. Sadly, I have no rights to live and work in the US, so it's back to Canada for me in 10 days! Not that that's a bad thing, of course. I'm yet to find a location to call home, but all in good time.

She wrote back the next day:

Nice to have an update. I was thinking the other day when you hadn't posted anything on IG as to how do I tell when I should be 'worried'? As in, you are a solo traveler who obviously doesn't want to be checking in every five minutes, but if a week goes by without anything would that be cause for concern? What if you were abducted and trapped in a hut in the middle of nowhere by some random stranger who's taken your phone and you cannot communicate! Can I suggest we come up with something that will not be a pain but could be good for both of us? Not sure what but maybe an IG post at least every three days? One pic shouldn't be too hard unless you're going off grid then advance warning is fine. Open to suggestions. :-)

Sorry if that seems a bit 'dark' but I have to look out for you.

I never got my mum's email.

By the time it landed in my inbox I was already facing my first night in the canyon.

NEW ZEALAND

My mum had wanted to call me Jessica. *Jessica Claire.* A strong name for a strong daughter. Dad didn't really fancy the Jessica part, but he liked Claire.

'Nice and simple,' he'd reckoned.

My mother wasn't entirely convinced that nice and simple was strong enough for the daughter she was anticipating, but she relented.

For better or worse, their parenting style was very much 'do what makes you happy, but we want you to figure it out on your own'. I think my mum, in particular, was afraid of having a daughter who didn't know how to stand on her own two feet. She wanted to make sure I could take care of myself. The idea that I would go through life relying on other people was a dangerous prospect. That this would leave me vulnerable, without power. I had to learn to fend for myself for my own good.

'Obviously,' she would go on to tell me, 'I didn't have anything to worry about.'

We grew up, for the most part, on the New Zealand seafront. Our little home with its faded blue weatherboard seemed so small among the other houses, but it managed to fit the five of us: my parents, my big brother, my little brother Chris and me. What's more, we had the beach just steps from the front door. Throw a pebble from the porch and – if you got it over the sea wall – you'd hit sand. Our school years were sealed in a whirl of wind, salt and sand, serenaded by the shrill cry of seagulls and the soft, breathy sound of the waves rolling in. We got our bare feet dirty, toes and knees constantly grazed, building forts up in the bush tracks and in the sand dunes just along the beach. Setting traps in the flax and the cutty grass. Home videos of Chris and I show us in our coloured helmets wobbling off on our bikes to school. We had so much freedom growing up beside the sea. But just like the ocean, there was a lot below the surface.

There was an unpredictability in my older brother that could be very hard to live with. 'Behavioural issues' was the term that got used most. Whatever that meant. It was a vague, powerless term used to describe the rage that could appear like a tidal wave on a calm sea, seeming to come out of nowhere, and for reasons I will probably never understand. Everything about it frightened me. The force of it, the destruction he had, many times, proved capable of, and the not knowing when it might hit. I both feared and revered my big brother, but living with him was to live on constant alert. And it wasn't something our family discussed in great depth. My dad's language was humour. My mum's was stoicism. None of us spoke in vulnerability. Maybe it was the time we lived in, or the place – that New Zealand 'harden-up' mentality that seems to flow through the bloodstream. Or, maybe this is how it is for everybody, and part of what it is to be human. Either way, sitting down and talking about our feelings didn't come naturally. We just got on with it.

Getting on with it meant wearing the tension in our home like a cloak; sometimes it was so thick I thought I could see it, and if I reached out I would slice through it with my hand. It took up so much space that I had to fight to carve out some room for myself. I had my own bedroom at least, and Dad installed a lock on the inside of my door, so I could shut out the provocation of my big brother. In the end, though, I was shutting myself in.

Growing up in New Zealand felt so limiting. So small. As a teenager, I grew to resent what I felt were limitations on my great ambitions. What on earth could I achieve on this tiny island? How would I ever be seen and heard here? Living in New Zealand felt like exile. *The arse-end of the world*, as I'd often describe it. Like a lot of teenagers, I had bigger ideas for myself, and I wanted more than I felt it was able to give me. I was sequestered here so far from all the cultural references and exciting far-flung corners of the globe that I dreamed about. Those were the places meant for me. And as long as I was down here on this island, they would always be so far out of my reach.

To a bored, frustrated teenager in the arse-end of the world, London was *it*. It was the epicentre of all that was cool and creative, and possible. It was the home of the music, literature and films I devoured and, in my mind's eye, a place practically spilling over with opportunities. Above all, London represented a different life. I would get giddy thinking about what I could be there. *Who* I could be there. I could start anew. Leave all preconceived and outdated notions of who I was behind and be a better version of me.

And, more than a decade later, I had become that version. I had grown, and found direction, and London had not only fed me, it had sustained me. Roles had changed, friends had moved away, romances had come and gone, chapters had opened and closed... and London remained, steadfast and concrete. The only constant. I leaned on that. I leaned on London so much that by the time the anxiety and emptiness crept up on me, I convinced myself that as long as I was in London I was not alone...that being part of the scenery meant I was a part of something, and that this was enough.

As always, I ignored the nagging, empty feeling that I might be wrong about that. And that yet again, I was shutting myself in my room.

Dehydration is a god-awful business. One of those sensations that you have to experience to really appreciate how agonizing it is. Dehydration is so much bigger than thirst, which is merely the first sign that hydration is running a little low. Thirst is a polite nudge, a warning. The sensation of being thirsty is also a lag, like light following sound, and if you feel thirsty, it's a sign that dehydration has already begun. I had been rationing what water I had left, but I was down to the last half-litre and already suffering the effects of not having enough.

It starts in the mouth, the initial pang of craving quite subtle and easy to ignore, but the signals get more insistent. Over time your tongue becomes increasingly dry and scratchy, thickening like a woollen mitten, rasping against the sides of your mouth, almost sticking to it like Velcro...From there you feel it in your head; a slowly increasing pressure throbs inside your skull, as if your brain is slowly shrinking in on itself, withering like a piece of dried fruit.

You notice your heart is beating faster as the body speeds up its cardiac output and restricts the blood vessels, trying to keep enough blood pumping through your system. It prioritizes the internal organs above all else so your skin, rationed of blood, gets clammy and cool, and you get chills, even in the searing heat. Your eyeballs become sapped of moisture and feel gritty and heavy inside their sockets. A twisted pain flares up your side, which is a sign that the kidneys are starting to parch. Left too long, the organs will run down one by one. This is ultimately how you will die.

As the body struggles, so does the mind. It becomes harder

and harder to concentrate, hazy spells of dizziness come and go, all physical strength depleting so that even turning your head can make you feel faint. And as you go on denying the body what it's begging for, the mind attempts to send urgent messages via desperate tricks of the imagination. Mine abused me with a vivid fantasy slideshow of refreshments that I could not make real.

Chilled water. The clink of ice cubes in a glass. Row upon row of bottles in the style of a limitless vending machine: label-less bottles of fizzy liquid in pale, translucent pastel colours, their curved glass dewy with condensation, drops slipping slowly down the sides. I thought about a can of Diet Coke – heard the crack and hiss as the can was opened, imagined the bubbles fizzing against my tongue, as refreshing as anything I'd ever tasted. It was the greatest torture. The longing, the desperate need of it, the very thought of a cold drink, even for a moment, was physically painful.

Back in the car, a spare bottle of water sat in the cupholder, just behind the gearstick. It was Natalie's flask which I'd borrowed from the house, designed to keep chilled beverages cold. I could see it now, its silver lid glinting in the sun. Awaiting my return. Keeping that water cold. My post hike refresher.

I would think about that bottle a lot.

It had been such a last-minute, spur-of-the-moment decision to leave that extra litre of water behind. From the house I'd brought the three-litre CamelBak, the Thermos bottle and my plastic-handled one, five litres in all. Once at the trailhead, about to lock up the car, I'd had a little idea: rather than carry all of the water in with me, I'd leave one behind. That way I could drink what I took during the hike and still have a cold drink waiting for me when

I got back to the car. What a clever plan, I'd thought, imagining coming back from the trail tired and sweaty, having finished the lukewarm dregs of my CamelBak, and being able to enjoy a whole bottle of still-cold water for the drive back to town.

I was kicking myself now. I could have easily slipped it into the daypack; there was ample room, I'd not packed much at all, and to think if I had it now...

Well for one, I wouldn't be forced to do what I did next.

I was about to run out of water. And right there beside me was a substantial source of liquid. My bottle of urine.

It was not a decision I had ever expected to make.

But it wasn't a difficult one.

There are various theories about drinking urine. Many insist you shouldn't. That doing so will only dehydrate you further. And because it's a waste substance, the very stuff the body rejected, consuming it for long enough is only going to recycle it to a point where it would become toxic. And sure, I believe this to be true. But when death by dehydration looks pretty certain, risking possible renal failure seems the better gamble.

Somewhere in the back of my mind were vague, faded-newsprint recollections of stories about people lost at sea or deep in the jungle who had survived by drinking their urine. Had I remembered that right? It was awareness that seemed stuck somewhere in the recesses of my brain, like chewing gum to the bottom of an old school desk – too long ago to place, but very much solidly there. And I definitely remembered reading a lifestyle article many, many years ago, about people who drank their own urine for 'health benefits'. I still remember the photograph; a woman proudly holding the special jug she collected her wee in. I remembered how viscerally grossed-out I'd been.

And yet...here we were. Regardless of whether a person should drink urine, I knew a person *could*. And that was good enough for me. My water was almost completely gone, the last of it sloshing around in the bottom of the CamelBak. It wasn't going to be long before urine was all I had. I was facing a very serious reality and, in that, I had one choice. Drink my urine and die, or don't drink my urine and die.

Let's face it.

I didn't have a lot to lose.

But before I ran out of water completely, I had to make sure... could I stomach it?

I pinched my nose with one hand and, with the other, brought the bottle to my mouth, letting the thick, red plastic spout rest against my bottom lip. *OK. Here goes nothing.* Slowly, slowly, I tilted my head back, lifting the bottle with it, and let the amber-coloured liquid flow towards my mouth. Lukewarm urine trickled onto my tongue and down my throat. Pinching my nose harder, I swallowed.

My face screwed up, disgusted.

It was bitter, slightly acrid.

It was disgusting.

I released my nostrils and took a gulp of air, which is when I was hit with the vile aftertaste – something I can only describe as the nostril-curling scent that wafts through the door of a men's public toilet. Only this was in my nose, concentrated in the back of my sinuses. I gagged. But I didn't retch, and what this meant was that I knew I could physically keep it down. Taking a tiny sip of my precious remaining water to wash away some of the horrid taste, I accepted my new number one task: keeping that bottle as full as I could.

I lay there, feeling a tiny sense of relief that I might be able to keep myself going a little longer.

[video]*No one came. It's so hot – I've half a litre of water left, I've been rationing it.* [pause] *I've started drinking my own urine, which is absolutely revolting, but...it should help me get by. I keep fantasising about an ice-cold can of Diet Coke. Oh my god. Several times I've thought, 'Fuck it, I'm going to deal with the pain –* [licks lips] *sorry, my mouth is so dry – deal with the pain and just get up and just slog on. But oh my god. I've tried. And I had to stop because the pain gets so excruciating that I think I'm going to pass out. I'm so thirsty...My water's basically gone...It's so scorching, and I'm now already into my bottle of piss. Which is strangely refreshing. Nobody's coming to look for me and that's what's really frightening. Because if someone comes and finds me, I'll be fine...But if I go through one more hot day like this I'm a goner. I've got no more resources. My kidneys hurt, I'm dehydrated...*[picks up bottle of dark-orange liquid and holds up to camera]*This is the colour of what I'm drinking, which just kinda says it all really. It's not how I want to go, I have to say. Really hoping someone finds me.*

In time I felt a shadow creep over my face and noticed the sun was finally moving behind the thumb-shaped rock above me, bringing as much relief as one can get when baking in the desert heat. The shift made me feel released, like I had been holding my breath all day. Over the next couple of hours the shadow would make its way down my body, until eventually I was left in the sweet, cool reprieve of shade.

It was bittersweet though. The arrival of shadow, and the imminent departure of daylight, meant I was sliding towards evening. If nobody had come past by now, it meant that nobody was coming past at all today. I would need to brace myself for another long night.

No, no, please no...

Not another night.

I can't take another night out here

The cold and lonely hours loomed large ahead, a gaping yawn of blackness, and I felt a cold, clammy fear sinking into the gaps around my ever-diminishing optimism.

One night was an unfortunate experience; two nights was something else.

But, dead or alive, the world keeps on turning and now the night was rolling in. I had got myself into this mess. And was going to have to accept the fact I might not get out.

Here, in this canyon, I was as vulnerable as I had ever been. And in that moment, when I really needed to ask for help – and was ready to – I found I could not reach out to anyone. Nothing to appeal to but the ancient rocks around me and the endless sky above, nothing but the hawks that circled overhead to hear my pleas. I thought of all the times I had skirted around opportunities to let people in and kept people at arm's length. Every time I camouflaged my needs and vulnerabilities in a bid to seem stronger, I only fed the isolation that would eventually devour me.

Perhaps it served me right.

The familiar shroud of chill sank into the canyon and, with it, the terror of darkness. It was big darkness – so large, so endless, that if it wasn't for the sheets of stars it would be difficult to tell where the earth ended and the sky began. They filled the sky, so many of them, layers upon layers upon layers.

It was impossible to see them without thinking of the many nights spent with my mum and stepdad, drinking wine, and on how many occasions we would wind up lying out on the lawn, stargazing. It always seemed like a good idea at the time.

'Tony, put on Don McLean!' Mum would shout to my stepdad, flat on her back in the grass, and soon the melody of 'Vincent (Starry Starry Night)' would come tumbling out of the windows of the house as we stared up into the night sky, saying nothing. We might not be a cuddly kind of family, but we can be incredibly sentimental.

Whenever I was in New Zealand I'd always look for the Southern Cross, only visible from the southern hemisphere. It was like a special code, signalling that I was home. Out here, the stars were different. I was so far away from anywhere familiar. But there were more stars tonight than I had ever seen before. Don McLean played quietly in my mind. The blackness was so deep, and so rich with sparkles and flares, so layered, I felt like I could fall into it, and swim. Or drown in it.

I looked for shooting stars. And saw one.

Two.

Three.

I wished on every single one of them.

In truth it felt more like begging.

Please.

Day Three: Thursday

Dawn. The sky was still a pale shade of grey, but I could already tell the day was going to be a hot one. It was palpable even as the first rays of light speared the valley, the air thick and heavy, the sun cutting a path through it like a spoon through treacle. My reserves were worn so thin already, and with the temperature playing this heavy hand this was a battle I was set up to lose.

Discomfort had reached a vicious peak: my kidneys groaned, my broken bones felt hot under my skin and blistering sores had formed on the backs of my heels where they continued to press against my boots. The urge to roll over was immense. Everything was screaming out for respite. But while my body struggled, my mind sought out possibilities of rescue. They were tiny, but I was sure they were there, like feeling little tugs on a fishing line. They kept me focused even at my lowest ebb and my head on the task of surviving. It was woefully threadbare hope, but hope nonetheless.

One thread of hope I was holding on to was the fact it was now Thursday. Time was edging tantalizingly close to the weekend, the point when – I told myself – there were sure to be more people in the park. Joshua Tree got plenty of visitors every day of the week, but especially so Friday through to Sunday when the day trippers and weekenders advanced on the park in their droves for hikes and rock-climbing and sightseeing. And so, I figured that as the number of visitors peaked, the chances of my being found would surely increase.

Even though this wasn't exactly a tourist trail that I was currently on.

Even though I wasn't currently on a trail at all.

I tried not to dwell on that.

The other thread of hope had even more potential: I had plans tonight.

In theory, I was supposed to be going out with Alison that evening. Last Sunday afternoon a drink at Mesa Bar had turned into an impromptu dinner with her and Bryan at a local Mexican restaurant, tucked into a vinyl booth decked out in garishly painted landscapes and walls of bright reds, yellows and blues. Over cheap tacos and micheladas, Alison had suggested she and I spend Thursday night out at The Palms in Wonder Valley – another rugged desert bar she had sung high praises about. The Palms was, I was told, more lively and more remote than Mesa Bar; so remote that we'd probably need to camp the night there in her van. Remote desert bar? New friends? Van camping? Yes! I'd been madly excited about this plan – and now, it could be my lifeline.

Sure, it had been a tentative plan, made almost on a whim. But still. It was something. It meant there was cause for someone to reach out to me. Purpose. Alison would be likely to text me about firming up arrangements. And that's when my lack of response might be noticed. That's when the touch-paper of my search and rescue might somehow, at last, be lit.

When you're trying to hang on to hope, the smallest strand will do. Anything that might float and keep you from drowning becomes a potential life raft; it doesn't matter how flimsy it is, if you can grab it, you will. I was a drowning sailor clutching at a straw.

Almost the weekend.

Alison might try to contact me.

People might have texted me.

Someone might notice I'm gone.

Hope. That was all I had to sustain me at this point.

But hope wasn't an easy thing to maintain. How long could a straw keep you afloat when you're in the middle of the ocean? How hard it felt, what with the heat, and the pain, and the days wearing on, to stay optimistic. A constant battle not to sink. And I was increasingly losing my grip.

I thought of my friends. I would have given anything, absolutely anything, to be sitting around talking about the most dumb-ass things with them – with all or any one of them. Just one more stupid conversation. One more round of laughing about something. Of taking the piss out of each other. God, that might just be what I missed the most.

This is your own fault.

You shouldn't have been such a loner.

You should have been a better friend.

You should have been a better person.

You failed.

This is your own fault.

I felt myself weaken. My grip softened and my fingers slipped from their hold on hope. I let it bob there on the surface, the waters eerily still, nothing moving, detached and afloat, and in that moment I felt completely adrift.

You might not get out of here, you know.

It's already been this long.

Nobody's noticed.

Too many things need to happen by chance.

Face it.

You are helpless.

And it is hopeless.

You are just riding out the end now.

I began to cry.

That thing I cannot do with any ease had finally happened; I had let go of trying to tough it out, of denying my vulnerability, and I had looked directly and unblinking at the thing I had been trying my hardest not to focus on all this time. The end of my life. The end of all I had ever done, and ever known, and ever felt. It would soon be over. And for what? What legacy had I left behind? Had I ever made any impact on anyone? Had I done enough? Had I done it well? Had I done anything of value? Had I let people know honestly that I loved them as much as I did?

Crying was a release, and it was an admission of sorts. I'd finally admitted to myself how fucking afraid I was.

Perhaps it was time I admitted this to the people I will never see again.

[video] *This is the first time I've actually cried because I'm getting really freaked out now. And I just think of all of you guys, my friends and my family, and...I'd do anything to see you guys.* [sobbing] *I don't wanna be here...I really don't want to be here. I guess I should find some hope in the fact I still have tears, so I'm not completely dried up yet. Oh god. There's still hope, there's still hope...I'm just feeling a little bit freaked out.*

Even now, I was still fighting it, struggling with exposing my absolute fear and devastation. And at the same time, still clinging on to that hope, that sodden straw. *I'm just feeling a little bit freaked out.* Day three of impending death in the middle of a desert and I still felt the need to put my brave face on. Although this time I think it was for me.

If you'd ever asked me what I would do in such a situation, armed with a camera, I would have said with great certainty that I'd record in-depth, personalized messages for those I loved. But I didn't do that. I didn't do the thing I expected, to open my heart in earnest. Not because I didn't have things I wanted to say, or because I didn't want to say them…But because I refused to accept this was it.

Recording my goodbyes and smashing open the piggy bank of my emotions would mean giving in and beginning a process of accepting my fate. So, no. It was not getting in, none of it, no white flag, no reality check, *nada*. I refused to take my brave face off. That same mechanism that had kept me locked in my own emotional panic room for so long was not budging even now. While that brave face had been problematic before, here and now, in many ways, that refusal kept me going.

Harden up.

God, I can be a stubborn fucker.

Old habits die hard. But so, it seems, do I.

———

The early afternoon crawled into view. The sun was now directly on top of me and the heat was having a serious effect on my mind and body. It was a relentless battle that I began to realize I was losing. Every time I felt reinvigorated by an injection of hope, the heat would beat me backwards: one step forward, two steps back. As I suffered the burn, the flames of my desperation grew higher. And today the heat was the worst it had been so far. I was struggling to cope.

Shading my face from the sun, I switched on the camera once more. Now, I was pleading. Pleading and bargaining.

[video] *I'm cooking here. Fuck. I don't understand why no one's looking for me...It's Thursday, there might be walkers on this trail on Saturday, maybe? I don't know if I'll survive that long. But why is no one looking for me? I'm trying to cover up as much of me as possible, any little bit of me in the sun is literally cooking. I've got a few cooked patches on my legs. But you know what? If I have to...lose my legs then fine, I just want to get out of here alive... Taste a cold drink...See my friends and family again...Where is the search party? Where is everyone? This is day three.* [Camera moves to urine bottle] *I've got that much disgusting stuff left to survive on, plus whatever else I can manage to get out of myself. Jeez.* [Whispers] *Please, please, come soon.'*

To be honest, I no longer knew who I was talking to – myself, mostly. The little black camera had become a journal of sorts. I needed to talk. To have a voice. I was going mad out here, suffering the heat and sapped of patience. Funny; I'd almost brought my journal with me, the morning I was packing for this hike, thinking that once I reached the oasis I would have lunch in the shade of the palms and write about the trail...a romantic notion that at the last moment I decided was unlikely and wholly unnecessary.

Leave it, you can write about it when you get home.

I supposed people would find my journal. It was not written for others to read, yet now they would and I wondered what they would make of my mind's ramblings. The last entry I had written was the Sunday before I set off for the Lost Palms Oasis. I'd shared excited tales of the weekend: a glorious morning hiking with Alison; getting my ear pierced and getting to know the folks at the tattoo shop; the convivial evening with Jo and Jef and their friends...Enthusiastic, contented pages about being in the desert, loving the freedom of driving, meeting new people, feeling so connected in a way I hadn't been for a very long time.

I was, to use my own written words, 'deliriously happy'. It was a post full of love.

Driving the desert roads in my hat, shorts and boots and blasting the radio, the desert and the Joshua trees all around me, heading to one of my favourite local spots, I feel happier in my own skin than I have since...I can't remember.

It was a nice note to go out on, I suppose.

Except...

Fuck that.

There it was, that spark of stubborn anger. What a relief to know it wasn't completely extinguished. That cantankerous Claire, the pissed off one, feeding off a deeply buried rage, she was still in there, burning away. How could things end just when they were getting so good? I had come so far! I had worked so hard to get through my mess, figure my life out. And I had finally got to this point, only just dipped my fucking toe into a life that was serving me better, and discovered where I needed to go! And these connections, these experiences...I finally felt like I was on the right road after all this time! THIS WAS JUST THE BEGINNING.

And there was no way I was giving it all up without a damned good fight.

But as the heat intensified and my strength slowly ebbed away into nothing, my thoughts seemed to fling themselves aimlessly around in my brain, like a fly hurling itself at a window. I squinted up into the dark shape of my sunshade, making out the white-purple glow of the sun through the top of my hat. What time was it? *What day was it?*

'It must by Thursday. I never could get the hang of Thursdays,' I said out loud to myself. It was a throwaway line from the *Hitchhiker's Guide to the Galaxy*. Remembering it amused me, and it was nice to feel amused in the thick of all this; it meant my spirits were still working hard to stay up. Humour had always helped when times were difficult. *Especially* when times were difficult.

Laughter is the cure for tension, and I had taken it upon myself quite early in life that it was my job to make other people feel more at ease. I was often trying to be funny. I'd write humorous comics and poems for family birthday cards or in notes passed to friends in class. And now here I was, trying to do the same for myself.

I never could get the hang of Thursdays.

It was my obsession with Radiohead that lead me to read *The Hitchhiker's Guide*. My friend Liz had given me a valuable piece of information one day during class, seeing the band's photos all over my sixth form workbook.

'You do know the name *OK Computer* comes from *The Hitchhiker's Guide to the Galaxy*, right?'

'The what-now?'

'It's a book. Well, a few books. It's a trilogy of five,' she added, chuckling to herself. I didn't get the joke at first, distracted by this new jewel of Radiohead information.

'What's it about?'

'It's sci-fi. Sort of. That's where the name 'Paranoid Android' comes from too.'

I conceded that if it was good enough for Radiohead, I had to have it.

Liz loaned me her copy and I devoured it on my bus ride home – so much so that I missed my stop. I found author Douglas Adams's deadpan humour and observations of human behaviour to be brilliant and utterly compelling. As a fifteen-year-old, I felt I was in on some wildly intelligent joke and I grew as fanatical about *The Hitchhiker's Guide* as I had about Radiohead. My favourite character was Ford Prefect: an intergalactic travel writer from another planet, posing as an out-of-work actor from Guildford. It was my dream to be a travel writer, living in England, and the fact he was a little different, a little misunderstood, a character who felt he wasn't extraordinary and yet didn't entirely belong...I thought I had actually found myself in something.

Getting from high school to home required two trains, and the commute was my time, where I could lose myself in thought, staring out the window as the carriage shunted gently around the curve of the wind-slashed harbour. My yellow plastic Walkman whirred through cassettes of songs I'd taped off the radio, the order so familiar that I could anticipate where the DJ cut it off at the end well before it happened. *There are big things ahead for me*, that's what I'd tell myself. I fantasized about the places I'd go...I imagined being in London and what it would look like, being so close to the bands and the writers and the actors I looked up to. *Breathing the same air!* Thinking about what was ahead of me could elicit a physical twinge of excitement. I was a daydreamer, but I felt like optimism was the great superpower that would get me where I needed to go.

The same year I discovered *Hitchhiker's Guide*, our college installed its first student computer room, and thus the girls of Sacred Heart were introduced to The Internet. Each of us was issued with an official school email address that incorporated both our name and the full name of the college, some 32 characters long and ludicrously cumbersome.

None of us had developed any context for the world wide web – to begin with, I used it mostly to do homework (a bit), and search for photos of bands to print out and stick in my school planner (a lot). But curiosity had drawn me further into its depths. The novelty of emailing my friends from across the room had quickly worn off and I decided to send my first unsolicited email to a stranger on the internet. I would write to Douglas Adams. His website was easy to find and, sure enough, there was an invitation to contact the author in England.

I didn't *actually* think my email would go to Douglas Adams. If I'd known I might actually connect with someone I idolized, I would possibly have written something more sensible. But teenagers are not only far too sure of themselves and blithely compulsive, they will avoid embarrassment like the plague. Why write a heartfelt message in earnest if I turned out to be wrong? *Pffft, I knew it wasn't really him.* I kept it cool.

Excuse me, sir, but I have to ask you a question?

I have decided I am Ford Prefect and I want to officially, legally and socially change my name to that. I ask your permission. Being a question, you may answer no.

Please?

The very next day at lunchtime, I logged into my account and sure enough there was a response from the email address of Douglas Adams. I stared at the unread message in my inbox. I wasn't sure I'd actually expected a reply. Is this really how this world wide web thing worked? Was it that simple? Could I really have received a message from the great man himself?

I had.

It's not something you need my permission for. You may want to ask around your friends and also perhaps your professional medical advisors, before you make such a step.

Best, Douglas Adams.

Elation. Wonder. Possibility. This was the moment I realized the power of the internet, that by being online I was in touch with the universe. That there was so much possibility for connection – I could reach out and tap the shoulder of absolutely anyone. Maybe here I could be seen and find a place in the big wide world I so desperately wanted to join. Who knew that over time it would only become another wall to hide behind?

Lying there in the dirt, I wondered what teenage me would have thought about the way it wound up ending for us. Would she even have chosen to believe it? I felt desperately sad for her, to think that everything she ever did, all she went through, all she experienced, was only going to lead to her dying in this damned hole.

I wished I could give her a message. Tell her I wasn't ashamed of her. That I had forgiven her for not being quite what she wanted and accepted that she was a lot of extraordinary things. To tell her she didn't need anyone else's validation – she could give it to herself.

I wished I had given it to her.

You are good enough.

You are going to hesitate all the time because you're afraid to fuck up.

Go forth and fuck up, my girl.

Fuck up like there's no tomorrow.

Needless to say, though, this was not the fuck up I'd had in mind for her.

And granted, our tomorrows might indeed have run out.

It then occurred to me that there was another piece of advice from Douglas Adams, one I could really use. It was, of course, that famous phrase that appeared on the cover of *The Hitchhiker's Guide to the Galaxy* itself: Don't Panic.

Easy for him to say.

LONDON

I woke up exhausted. Again. Everything hurting. Again. Situation normal: all fucked up. I rolled on to my back, shoved off my duvet and felt the twinge of familiar pain from both wrists, stiff in their grey plastic casts and strapped up with Velcro. This had been going on for almost two years now. I was still waiting to get used to it, so I could get on with things. But it had only got worse. It had become my most reliable and constant companion.

The pain that had plagued my wrists had expanded its territory: today I was going to a physio session for my back. I'd already had hand therapy at the hospital on Monday morning. In fact, I'd been seeing the hand therapist so frequently that my appointments had started feeling like a catch-up with a friend. I'd bring her copies of the magazine and we'd share restaurant recommendations, recipes and stories from our weekends. We could have been two pals chatting at a bar. Instead, the only bar between us was the stainless steel one she dragged hard across my tendons in a bid to unknot them. There were warm gel baths, physical exercises, and – always – new strips of tape applied, running from my thumbs to the elbow crease of my forearms.

Physio for my back was the latest addition to my weekly routine. It wasn't something I looked forward to – I didn't get any relief from it – and today, particularly, I felt a complete and absolute reluctance to go. I had come to hate the physio, all of it, and as far as I could tell the pain wasn't going away. Nevertheless... it had to be done.

No doubt it was the pain and the shitty sleep that were making me cranky.

I felt perpetually cranky.

I went through the motions of showering and dressing and dragged myself to the hospital, taking the usual lift to the second floor and sitting in my usual seat in the waiting area between the table of dated *National Geographic* magazines and the fake plastic tree, by this point seething and emotional. I felt I might cry at any moment...one prod could burst me like a balloon. Every part of my body tensed up, holding it in. *Just get on with it.* I would just get through the appointment and then get on with my day.

Ten minutes later, I was on all fours on the physio examination table in just my jeans and bra, where Priya, the effusive physiotherapist, was trying to bend me, contorting me into different shapes in an attempt to manipulate my spine.

'Cat!' she sang, as I arched my back. 'Now, cow!' as I inverted my back the other way. 'Cat! A little more, lift your spine a little more...'

'I can't,' I muttered, grimacing as the pain in my back twinged and my wrists threatened to crumple. 'It doesn't go that way.'

I'm not a bloody cat.

It wasn't Priya's fault. She wasn't to know there was probably more to all of this than a tight posture from too much desk work. It was me, this was all me. I had become completely out of balance on the inside and now it was finding its way to the outside. But not being able to fix it, despite all the help I was getting, made me feel so utterly pathetic and hopeless and frustrated that it took all my willpower to fight off tears. I was not going to cry, not here.

Let's just get this over with.

Being weak and vulnerable is not a comfortable fit for anyone, but it was certainly a position I could absolutely not bear to find myself in. Every single day someone would enquire, kindly, after my wrists, and I really wished they wouldn't. I was embarrassed to have a weakness that drew attention. Ashamed to have a weakness at all. Ashamed to be *weak*.

Priya now had me lying face down on the bench, my cheek pressed against the over-sanitized vinyl bench, a pillow inelegantly stuffed under my ribcage, when I heard her suggest that I should start sleeping like that: on my stomach, propped up with a pillow.

'That should alleviate the back pain at night,' she said in her sing-song voice.

Surely she wasn't serious. So was this me for the rest of my life now? I gritted my teeth and thought of my plastic wrist casts. The straps of physio tape that currently ran up both arms and formed an X shape across my shoulders. All these craft-box attempts to get this pain in my body managed. All the things I was already trying. I felt so pathetic.

Can't I just be normal?

I longed to move, and sleep, and not have to make all these specialized considerations for a pain that has no obvious cause and doesn't seem to be going away.

Priya must have seen the expression on my face; her already kind eyes softened further and she told me she would refer me to (yet) another specialist who could prescribe me some anti-inflammatory pills. But the idea of going to another medical professional only made me want to scream. To scream and scream and scream until there was nothing left inside of me.

Instead I just said: 'OK.'

As I walked out of the automatic doors of the hospital my body was still hurting but on the inside I felt completely numb. I now had to walk a few blocks down to the other hospital in Mile End to collect some orthotics for my shoes. The foot specialist I'd been referred to thought maybe it was a lack of foot support causing poor alignment, creating a domino effect of pain and tension in my body...So many theories for symptoms without a cause.

I appreciated the determination of doctors to find a solution, but I felt like everyone was guessing and somewhere along the way I had slipped into a numb state of autopilot, moving through the motions.

It fought a strange battle within myself: on the one hand so certain I was capable of dealing with everything on my own – irritatingly, stubbornly so – and feeling very strongly about the fact that being an independent woman was the flag I flew. The very idea of needing another person to help me through weakness actually pained me with shame. But at the same time, I wanted so badly to have someone to lean on in these moments, someone who could help take the strain of the little aches, to give me a hug at the end of a long day, after the drip-drip frustration of hospital appointments and constant low-level pain. Saying this to anyone was not an option. They'd think I was saying I wished I was in a relationship, and that wasn't it at all. Nice as that would be, I squirmed at the notion of needing one. It was simply that I needed these emotional supports and I couldn't seem to give them to myself. Even if I could admit this to anyone, I didn't really believe it was something I could call on someone else for. So it was much easier to deny the need entirely.

The thing about needs is that they can be ignored but they don't go away. They fester. And most of the time, they grow.

Two hospital visits done, I made my way to work. Slumped on the Central Line, my head leaning into the grubby glass partition at the end of the carriage, I counted down the stops to Oxford Circus.

Eight...Seven...Six...

Today, I could tell, was going to be difficult. My whole body was a tightly wound ball of emotion and it would take less than a prod to burst me open; in fact, I feared if anybody spoke to me, I would turn to water.

Five...Four...Three...

As the train doors opened at one stop or another, a class load of junior schoolchildren stampeded into the carriage, trampling each other for seats, squealing and jostling and laughing, the volume in the small space suddenly turned up. I was a balloon – fragile, at risk of bursting. I got off at the very next stop and moved to another carriage. It wasn't that I couldn't endure the squealing children so much as I didn't want the children to endure *me*, and my twisted, pent-up, emotion-chewing face. I didn't want to be around people. I wanted to be invisible. To disappear.

But in London you are never alone, even when you're lonely.

Arriving at the office, I caught my reflection in the lift's mirrored wall, rearranging my face into something that resembled normal. By some strange turn of fate, nobody else in my team was particularly chatty that morning; it was a rare moment of everyone being head-down and focused at their desks. The normal state of affairs was a buzz of conversation, everyone regaling each other with stories of home life, ranting about their commute or investigating various parcels sent in by PRs. I was surprised to find such a quiet, studious scene but, whatever the cause, I was thankful for it.

Because coming to work was a mistake.

The moment I sat down at my desk I knew it. I knew I wasn't all right. And that I had to get the hell out of there. But I couldn't just get up and leave, people would ask me things. And if I was going to hold myself together, I could not speak a word. Not. One. Word.

I pulled on my big headphones and pretended to busy myself in some edits, but in truth I was staring at nothing, listening to nothing, just clenching my jaw and trying to breathe and barely keeping it together.

The glass door to Emma's office was closed as she took a phone call. Our long-suffering deputy editor, recently promoted to editor – the new captain of our sinking ship. And my friend. My confidante. I watched her out of the corner of my eye, waiting for her to finish.

Emma had come into my life at a time when I was doubting everything about my abilities and helped me rebuild my self-belief. The universe works in mysterious ways and I'm still convinced she was sent to pull me back from the edge. Perhaps we both needed each other. After especially gruelling days at work, we'd leave the office together and walk, extending our commute by taking longer routes, unloading our mutual frustrations at London life, the growing sense of imbalance we were both feeling and the longing to spend more time in our happy places – for her, this was the ocean, and for me, wide open wilderness. I'd begun to muse out loud that maybe I'd pack it all in and move to Canada and live in a cabin. 'And find a kind-eyed lumberjack,' she would tease. We'd share these same ruminations often, and looking back I think just having those feelings acknowledged by someone who shared them made the imbalance more manageable.

Until now. Today I had something else to tell her, and I had to do it quickly. I sent her an email:

Em, I'm not OK. Do you mind if I go home?

I waited, every muscle clenched, for her to finish her phone call. I hoped she would just give me a nod, permission to go, and I could stand up and leave without a word needing to be said to anyone. But I knew that's not how this would go down.

She had already sensed something was up with me.

The week before we'd taken a lunchtime wander down Carnaby Street, wrapping our coats against the autumn chill. Emma's voice shifted in tone from our usual comical banter to one of gentle concern.

'Nels, I've been wanting to ask...' she stopped walking for a moment to look at me '...are you OK?'

'Me? Yeah...I'm fine.'

Stock response.

'Don't take this the wrong way,' she said, 'But lately you seem kind of...angry.'

My heart stopped short. She could see that? She could see this awful, irritable anger that's been following me around all this time? God, I thought I'd been hiding it so well. I had gone out of my way to keep it from everyone around me, holding it in. I wasn't comfortable with how I'd been feeling and was terrified that if I shared it with anyone then these feelings would mean something and they would somehow come to define the person I was. The fact that Emma had noticed it, and that it had been worrisome enough for her to mention it, was horrifying. The shame filled every vein in my body and I could not have felt more exposed than if I had been standing naked right there in the middle of the street. But she had seen it, a glimpse.

My emotion had come to the surface.

I saw her put the receiver down, look up, then move to open the door of her office. With a gesture and a concerned look she ushered me in, and just as she closed the door behind me I heard her utter the words again, 'Nels, are you OK?'

And then I fell apart.

There was nothing to stop it any more. The wave, spilling over. It all came out. The tears came, big gulping sobs, as I admitted to her the thing I'd been too afraid to say out loud: I am not OK. That I was sinking. That I had gone to the doctor a few days ago and had been prescribed antidepressants. That I didn't want to take them. That this terrified me. That depression wasn't *me*. It wasn't who I was. I wasn't prepared to accept it. That my life felt like a blur of hospital, work, then home, and when I was alone, I felt numb. That I didn't know how to manage it all. And that I was ashamed of that fact.

Emma stacked tissues up in front of me as the tidal wave poured out.

'It's not who you are,' she said. 'It's something you're feeling. Be kind to yourself, Nelson.'

I am not a crier. Any emotion that tried to flow out of me had a dense trash-pile of other, repressed emotions to get through before it could reach my eyes. Sometimes it could leak through the cracks, but most of the time the tears stayed hot, beneath the surface, unable to escape.

Given I was now full-on ugly crying on my editor's table, it was clear that the dam had burst.

'Take the meds,' she said. 'Think of them like the physio tape you use on your tendons – giving you a little bit of support while you heal. You don't have to do this by yourself. Sometimes we need all the help we can get.'

When I got home I crawled on to my bed and held the box of sertraline on my lap. And in spite of all the fear, in spite of what this might mean, how this might redefine the person I was, I took the medication. Because although I was reluctant, I really, really wanted to stop feeling whatever this feeling was. I'd never envisaged myself as a person who took antidepressants, but the person I had become wasn't someone I recognized either. This person crying at work, this wasn't me any more.

I wasn't really expecting it to happen at all, let alone as quickly as it did, but within 24 hours I felt like I'd been plucked out of quicksand and placed back on solid ground. I actually felt OK. What's more – and this is what really struck me the most – it made me realize I had not been OK for quite some time.

I could breathe again.

You little beauts.

Antidepressants made me feel like me again. Which is not something I ever thought I'd say.

OK. So perhaps I really couldn't get through this by myself. But things had to change. Now. My life had become completely off balance. I'd repressed things for so long and the signs had been creeping up. It had been a good couple of years since I had passed out on my bedroom floor, and in that time my life on the outside looked to be going in leaps and bounds, while inside I'd felt a growing sense of disconnection, of isolation, of fear, of exhaustion. Why? What had gone so inexplicably sour? How could I feel these things, how could I be depressed when my life was this good? Why couldn't I be happy with everything I had? Who the hell did I think I was?

But that's the thing. I knew who I was. And I'd neglected her. I'd denied her needs. Now they were festering. It was becoming clearer and clearer that I'd become a tightly wound ball of stress and frustration and fear and anger, and my mind and body were suffering for it.

We are never just one person. Fundamentally we're a bunch of different versions of ourselves, making up one glorious, multifaceted human of so many colours and shapes. Most people who know me are familiar with the external Claire, the outward one: confident, wry, the tough Kiwi who deals with stress using deadpan humour and a rant, who shuns searching for a relationship for the sake of one and grabs a one-night stand as the prerogative of the single independent woman, who has no qualms turning up to a party where she doesn't know anybody, who likes taking risks, who is stubborn to the point of being a pain in the arse, who relishes getting outdoors and heading for a trail, wading in rivers and getting covered in dirt, who isn't afraid of getting outside of her comfort zone. Who isn't afraid.

I knew this Claire. I was proud of her. And I credited her with getting me through life thus far, pushing forward, never giving in, being a determined creature and rubbing sticks together to reignite her own fire of confidence every time it went out in a puff of self-doubt. She did this despite the fact she didn't know what she was doing most of the time. That Claire was in control. That Claire had the gumption to talk her way into concerts as a teenager; that Claire moved to London without knowing anybody or having a plan. That Claire quit a well-paid job to doggedly pursue an opportunity to become a writer. I nourished this Claire and I encouraged her to carry on being out there.

That Claire was real, but she wasn't the whole person.

There was the other Claire.

The Claire who was desperate to be seen and heard. The one who longed for connection, love and affection. Who wanted to please – a way of keeping the peace. Who was pretty fucking afraid, a lot. And who overthought *everything*. The Claire who still looked outside herself for validation and approval. And who constantly tripped up on a blazing white-hot fear of being misunderstood.

The needs of this Claire made her weak. But by my own classification, not anyone else's. For so long I had seen her as needy, when in fact she was just a Claire who had needs. There is a difference.

Needs are valid, whether we want to admit to them or not. And that was where I'd been going wrong – ignoring the needs I wasn't comfortable with because they didn't resonate with the Claire I most wanted to be. Denying them, though, didn't make them go away. That 'weaker' Claire was just as necessary to me as the so-called stronger version of myself I was lovingly embracing and, by pretending her needs had nothing to do with me, I was only running away from myself, all this time.

No wonder I felt lonely. It wasn't for a lack of people in my life. Something was simply disconnected inside me. I didn't even know whether I was an extrovert or an introvert any more. Probably I was both. A nature guide I'd met on my travels once made the observation that I was 'an introvert wearing the mask of an extrovert'. And when she said it, I'd felt emotionally winded. How had she seen me? The internal Claire hiding behind the external Claire. And although I was both, only one was being allowed to exist.

Of all these versions of ourselves it feels natural to present the one we like best, while we hide, ignore or flat-out deny the ones we're less keen on. We are ashamed of them. And we shame them constantly. They exist only on a diet of shame, of fear, of denial. I had neglected this other Claire, pretending she didn't exist. Is it any wonder I no longer felt whole? That I felt empty?

It was a small detail, perhaps, but one thing I had come to recognize as fulfilling for both Claires was spending time in the outdoors. There was adventure and risk and dirt, but also peace and simplicity and nature. A chance to flex my muscles and a chance to clear my mind. And perhaps that's why I found it so satisfying: a whole need being met. Walks, hikes, forest, coast, breathing in, breathing out...a foundation that served both sides. This wasn't how I consciously thought about it; I just gravitated towards it. Sometimes I could get my fix with a short autumnal stroll through Hampstead Heath, feeling twigs snap beneath my boots and tasting the fresh air in my lungs. Other times – particularly when I managed to catch myself withdrawing into a pit of despondency – I would book a train to the outskirts of Greater London, pack a lunch and take myself on a day's walk somewhere in the countryside, say the North Downs.

Even better were the occasional, joyful weekends away with friends – to the blustery peaks of Wales, Cornwall's salty coast, the lushness of the Lake District. As far as I was concerned, it didn't matter where we went, or what we did, as long as it was outside. I was as happy walking the white cliffs of the south coast as I was leaping into a river gorge or clambering eagerly up the steep spine of Striding Edge to Helvellyn's snowy crest. Paddling canoes down the Thames through the Oxfordshire countryside in the pissing rain. Clambering around rocky Pembrokeshire coves looking for sea caves and filling our pockets with foraged blackberries on the walk back to the campsite. Pints of ale, the smell of gas-cooker bacon, a dry change of socks and feeling of being worn out in the best way possible.

I'd return from these trips filthy and dishevelled and completely renewed, my body as damp and weather-tattered as the canvas of my tent that I'd spread out messily in the bathtub to dry. I knew this was what I needed more of. My heart knew it, my brain knew it, my body knew it, and it wasn't long before the three got together and began sending me some serious messages.

The state of my wrist had become so untenable that the final solution was surgery. I'd never had surgery before, but it sounded simple enough – and all that mattered to me was that *finally* I would have relief. I was actually excited. Less exciting was the recovery period...I would require a month off work and, while many people would welcome the break, I worried about the increasing isolation that might creep in when I wasn't going into the office. This, however, I kept to myself.

My friend Telli had a few questions. It was a Sunday, which meant a catch-up over coffee.

'Who's going with you to the hospital?'

'No one. I'm taking an Uber.'

'An Uber? Don't be silly, I'll come and take you.'

'No, it's OK, the hospital is just up the road, it'll be a five-minute cab ride.'

Telli sat back in her chair and gave me a look that told me how ridiculous I was being. I was used to that look. She'd often tell me it was pointless to argue with an Iranian, and as she was the only Iranian I'd ever argued with, I had to believe it was true.

'No. You can't Uber yourself to surgery.'

'Sure you can!' I indicated my phone on the table. 'Click the app and a chariot awaits, easy.'

'I'm coming to pick you up.'

I waved her away. 'That's crazy, mate, it's so much further for you to come to me than it is for me to get to the hospital.'

For a moment I thought she might relent. In Telli I saw that familiar duality, fierce strength that cloaked a deep vulnerability. There were moments when I caught glimpses of that other Telli, but I think that, like me, she had learned how to hide that version away, kept out of sight like a lady's maid in *Downton Abbey*. I think we probably recognized that in each other.

'Then how are you getting home afterwards?'

I fiddled with my coffee cup.

'Uber.'

'I am coming to the hospital with you and I'm taking you home after.'

'Honestly...'

'You know there's no point arguing with me. That's what's happening.'

I knew I couldn't win this one. So I relented. And was secretly grateful that she insisted on offering the thing I would never,

ever ask for.

'OK. Thank you.'

For the rest of the day I faced an inner tug-of-war between the discomfort of having someone going out of their way for me and the unexpected warmth I felt by letting it happen.

When Telli pulled up outside my building in a taxi the morning of my surgery I was surprised how strange it felt to be escorted to an appointment for once. I couldn't remember the last time I had an escort for anything. But as I watched the morning drizzle slick across the taxi window I knew that despite my usual reflexes – wanting to flee, feeling indebted and guilty about this arrangement, this imposition – I was grateful. It felt nice to be taken care of. It was happening. I let myself sink into it, feeling a comforting cloak of kindness wrap around my shoulders. I didn't have to do this alone.

Dr Huang was my surgeon and one of the finest hand specialists in London. I could easily imagine her – tiny, masterful, with the wizened, deadpan expression of an ancient sage – sitting atop a mountain dishing out philosophical asides. I found it harder to imagine her dressed in scrubs and wielding a scalpel. However, she was a renowned wizard with the scalpel and I was glad for it. While I slumbered blissfully under anaesthesia she released my tendon from the inflamed stranglehold of its sheath, stitched it back up and bandaged the whole forearm, until it was just a thick stump with fingertips poking out. The arm was strung up in a sling and eventually I was free to return home, free to do nothing but rest up for four weeks.

Four long weeks.

I couldn't decide if I felt liberated or trapped.

Telli escorted me home, ushering me to bed and helping to install a hook on the wall above it from which to hang my night sling – a big purple foam burrito that would hold my arm upright as I slept. And Telli, as she is wont to do, readied herself to take on the role of nurse. To be (quite literally in this case) my right-hand woman.

'I'll stay here with you until tonight,' she said. 'Are you hungry? Do you want me to cook you something?'

I could have said yes. Let her cook me dinner, accept the company and care, recognize that it was done with love. But as it was, she had already spent the entire day sitting idly at my bedside with little to do and the idea that she would stick around just to wait on me seemed unnecessary. Actually, it made me uncomfortable, feeling like an imposition, I was only one arm down. I could still do things. Weren't there loads of people in the world with one arm who got on with things just fine? I could totally manage.

'Thank you, mate,' I told her. 'You've been amazing. But it's fine, I have a freezer full of meals and pre-chopped veggies, everything's all ready to go.'

It was true, I had made every preparation I could think of for a month of fending for myself one-handed. I'd bought pull-on bras that didn't require clasping. I'd lined up all my slip-on shoes and stowed away anything with laces. I'd bought a plastic sleeve so I could shower without getting my bandages wet. Everything was taken care of. There was no need for anyone to fuss.

I suppose deep down I was afraid that if I relied on someone else it would open up the door to disappointment, hurt and, ultimately, a loss of control. Better to know I can handle everything myself. There is safety in that.

Not that I was thinking about any of this at the time; I was only doing what came naturally to me. Taking care of business on my own.

'I'm happy to make you something, though,' said Telli, as we continued our push–pull. 'I'm here, and you've just had surgery, you should rest!'

With friends like mine, feeling lonely didn't make any sense to me. Looking back, not letting myself need them might have had something to do with it.

I finally managed to persuade her it was fine to leave me by announcing I was going to go to bed and have a sleep. My friend raised an eyebrow, not convinced I should be left alone just yet. But she knew me well enough to push back just enough; she supervised me getting into bed, helping me into my strung-up purple sling, plumping my pillows and adjusting my blankets, and, as she turned and gave me one last concerned face through the bedroom doorway, I recited my usual mantra of reassurance.

'Really. I'm fine.'

Impressive. Even wearing a sling, I could still keep my friends at arm's length.

———————

That month after my wrist surgery went by surprisingly quickly, especially considering most of that time was spent watching all seven seasons of *Mad Men* and – thanks, power of suggestion – learning to make whisky sours. Which was kind of tricky to do one-handed. Still, I felt pretty pleased with myself for having accomplished something. Because there wasn't much else to accomplish.

The anti-depressants had allowed me to keep a handle on things, my feet firmly on the ground, but there was still an emptiness that followed me around. Now that I didn't have my job to go to, it felt overbearing. Spending the time binge-watching DVDs was the best distraction I could come up with. However, as it turns out, sitting on the sofa drinking whisky in front of the TV in the middle of the day wasn't as much fun as it sounds.

I didn't have many visitors; I felt increasingly disinclined to ask anyone to stop by and anyone who did offer to make a house call was brushed off, mostly because that would involve having to put my sociable face on. The emptiness, the great burdening weight of it, made the sociable face feel too heavy to wear. And so life continued in its usual quiet shell of isolation, only this time lacking the reliable routine of human interaction I enjoyed when I was going into the office.

I guess the upside of having all this time off with nowhere to go, nothing to do, is it gave me the chance to think. And to reassess what the hell I was doing with my life. I had pursued a life that looked a particular way, and here I was, living in it. It looked just like I had hoped: a charming flat, in the city of my dreams; a job on a magazine and a growing freelance portfolio; a circle of friends; reasonably good health and no real obligations. Where did the anxiety come from? And why was it stopping me from being happy? I didn't know. All I knew is that I wasn't and for so long I had tried to be, and perhaps that was the problem. It was time to listen to the other Claire. She was tired of not being seen.

She was sick of being lonely.

Loneliness didn't look like I thought it would, though. Its guise is deceiving. No matter how many people I met, no matter how busy I kept and no matter how utterly fantastic my friends were, I would find myself feeling completely isolated in the most crowded of places. Why was that? What was happening to me? There were plenty of people in my phone contacts who, if I told them I was lonely, would most likely jump to my side in a flash. Who will read these words and wonder why the hell I didn't give them a call. But it wasn't as simple as that.

I didn't know how to reach out and ask for the things that I needed. And there was always the risk of admitting the need, putting the call out for company, and finding myself wanting. Besides, I wasn't convinced this feeling was something that could be solved with company.

Over time I had been trying to stretch that half-person into a whole, trying to make her cover the big gaping hollow where my vulnerable, shamed self should be. As such, I found it hard to wholly connect with anyone.

That's what loneliness really is: a lack of connection.

That much I figured out when I started going to therapy. This, at least, was one step I could take to try to unravel the mess that in my head. To figure out why I could feel so empty when I was living the good life. I'd kept my sessions hush-hush at first, and only after admitting it slowly to friends around me did I realize that almost *everyone* I knew was seeing a therapist. We were all trying to work our shit out. There was a great relief in knowing that none of us really had it all together.

It took a few false starts with different therapists to get to

Nathan. He was the one who saw me. The rest, I'd felt, had been trying to find the right box to put me in. And I would not allow myself to be put in a box. Instead, he helped me unpack things. I had gone to try and figure out my anxiety, because I didn't like what it was doing to me. I was impatient to find clarity. Nathan, however, seemed preoccupied with what was going on with my wrists. And I felt he was going off track.

Just what I need, another doctor playing at this guessing game.

'Listen,' he implored. 'Remember what you told me about your childhood? How you didn't talk about your emotions.'

'Uh-huh.'

'What did you do when you had all that emotion? You wrote.'

It's true. I was always writing. From the moment I knew how, I wrote stories – usually about cats, and pirates, or cats who were pirates...But ultimately, about impossible adventures and places I'd never been. And I'd almost always kept a diary. In high school, friends and I started a band, and while I was a rubbish guitar player I won a couple of lyric-writing awards in national competitions. Words, in one form or another, had always been my arena of comfort.

What Nathan had made me understand was *why*. That growing up there had been so much focus on my older brother that I didn't feel heard. The only space I could occupy safely had been my bedroom, where there was no one else to listen. So I had raged in the written word. When sent to my room in an adolescent strop, I'd scrawl out any frustration on the back of my bedroom door in felt-tip marker until eventually my dad, sighing resignedly, had to repaint the whole thing. What I wanted more than anything was to be seen and heard and was never quite sure how to achieve it. Writing became the greatest tool for both. I was prone to scribbling notes and letters to my parents, determined to get my side of the story across, demanding a retrial for misdemeanors. Hilariously earnest, passionate missives explaining the injustice of it all, slid under the door. My mum still has them, amused and baffled by this insistence that I get my point across no matter what. I didn't have a clue what it meant at the time, but in a way, this was me adapting. Through writing, I created an outlet. I'd found my voice.

And now, according to Nathan, I was going hoarse. He waved his hand in the air, as if he were writing on an invisible chalkboard.

'Look at that,' he'd said, indicating his hand. I knew, immediately, what he was getting at.

'You're writing,' I said.

'And which hand do you write with?'

I'd held up my right hand, encased in thick grey plastic.

'Where's your pain?'

I kept it held high.

Nathan lowered his arm and leaned forward, resting his elbows on his knees.

'When you repress your emotions, you repress everything.'

That my body was giving me signs of how much I was holding back made more sense to me than any of the other theories presented; even my most crushing cynicism was prepared to step aside for this one. I *was* repressed. My body was trying to tell me so. And I didn't listen. Now, my repression was sliding into depression.

So how could I change all this? If I was so emotionally blocked, how could I unblock myself? Where should I go from here?

'You need to find a way to let it out,' Nathan told me. He suggested getting back into physical exercise, but I felt too broken, too sore and long past having any motivation. That was beyond the capabilities of my terrible lack of self-discipline. I knew that what I needed was a change much bigger than my routine. There were needs I needed to meet, and knowing what I knew of myself, the only way to meet them was head-on.

But how?

The question began keeping me awake at night. What little sleep I was already getting became tangled up in existential uncertainty. As soon as the light was off, I was lying alone in the dark with a serious case of brain congestion and a whole load of 'what-ifs' spilling out of the cracks.

And lately they were getting persistent.

What if I just don't know how to be happy?

It used to be that I would feel bursts of joy at the smallest of things. I had been that way for much of my life – feeling excited about the 'what-might-be's. Small moments of imagining where my life might lead could leave me almost giddy with anticipation. But along the way I'd lost that quick spark of excitement. Now that I'd reached my destination, I was lost.

Is that all there is? And what was it all for?

Sometimes the thought of this made me feel immensely tired. Physically exhausted, emotionally hollow had become my normal and I couldn't quite work out how.

What if this is me for the rest of my life?

Me. Here. Nose to a screen. Coming home to my room in my flat, alone, pulling the solitude over me like a comfort blanket that was slowly smothering me and failing to sleep. Then getting up and doing it all over again. Keeping the image of my best self afloat at all times while I was drowning beneath it. The set looked good. The role sounded impressive. But it wasn't real. Not to me, not any more. I felt like I was constantly trying to keep the wheels turning, only to find it was a hamster wheel and I was having to run non-stop, run until my lungs burst, just to keep it going. And for what? To what end? Was I doing any of this for myself any more, or just to keep up the appearance for everyone else?

But what else are you going to do?

Once anxiety crept to the surface I began to understand that trying to just *get on with it* wasn't going to work for me. Anxiety was always poised, ready to knock me off my feet. It was fight or flight, and I was always poised to retreat. There seemed only one way I knew to reset it. Pack up, leave and start again.

'Have you ever considered playing the long game?' Nathan had asked. 'Invest in making a long-term plan for change, rather than suddenly leaping out into the unknown?'

Don't be ridiculous. That's not who I am.

So I knew what was coming. My subconscious had already begun whirring away with big ideas, sending me images like a brochure for a better life. Every night when I closed my eyes, waiting the arduous wait for sleep to happen, I was transported to the open road, surrounded by wild and varied landscapes – something resembling Canada – a concentration of fir trees, pines, deep valleys cut through with rivers and high mountains tipped in snow. Freedom, adventure and the great outdoors, seen through the frame of a car windscreen. In that vision I felt the liberation of being at the wheel and the joy of solitude in nature, rather than a weight of loneliness. In those quiet moments in bed I could almost imagine myself feeling physically lighter.

What if I just left all this behind and hit the road?

It was only a fantasy, of course. What was I going to do on the road? I couldn't even drive, for fuck's sake. I'd started taking lessons, but progress was slow, likely because I couldn't shake a deep-seated reluctance to become a driver. Driving meant sharing the road with people who could smash into me at high speed or side-swipe me into oblivion. It meant, ultimately, trusting other people not to kill me. I had this deep-seated worry that I'd wind up a road statistic, which I'd always felt would be a shitty way to go. But maybe it was time to stop making excuses, to feel the fear and do it anyway? I felt a twinge of something, then; a newfound sense of direction.

What if I just hurried up and got my licence?

No really...what if I just hit the road?

———

Heat. The heaviness of it. I began to drift in and out of the here and now. I was woozy with lack of water, with heat, with fatigue, with the constant adrenaline that surged through my bloodstream, necessary to keep the full force of pain at a manageable level. Somewhere in a far-off place I heard a sound in the distance.

A faint 'wee-ooh-wee-ooh', as delicate as dust on the wind.

A siren?

Could that really be an ambulance? I strained to listen, to hear through the thick haze of heat that seemed to blanket me. Every sound seemed muffled by my pulse throbbing in my eardrums. The desert was an eerily quiet place much of the time, nothing but the shuffle of the occasional breeze against the paper map stretched over my legs.

I'm sure I heard a siren.

Perhaps there is an ambulance coming...perhaps it is coming for me...perhaps someone is coming to rescue me...

My eyelids were heavy and half-closed. I turned my head to the side, staring into nothing. In my mind I was trying to recall how my location had looked on the GPS – there was a road that ran about two miles to the south of here. I strained my ears some more, craning for the sound to come again. But I couldn't hear anything beyond the silence of the valley.

So I guess there was no ambulance.

Even if one had been on that road I was probably too far away to have heard it.

My mind was beginning to play tricks on me.

OK, so I was going mad then.

I suppose that was bound to happen.

I squinted up at the rocks above me, which seemed to sway faintly in the heat.

Thirst.

My head.

Distraction.

I needed distraction.

I picked up the camera.

[video]'*The sun's hitting now, coming into the "roast-lamb" stage of the afternoon. But this time I've smothered myself in factor 60*

[I held the tube towards the camera like an informercial] – *don't leave home without it...Including my legs, which I've covered with the help of the magic stick. And hopefully they won't incur too many more burns. Oh, I just wish I could get up and walk...*

I was rambling now. Desperate. I see myself on the video falling back into wry humour, hiding my weaknesses, putting other people at ease. Putting myself at ease. But those few who have seen all my videos are the people that know me. The people who understand that my brand of vulnerability still comes with deadpan jokes and withheld tears. That is still real, and it is me to the bitter end.

[video] *So, my mouth feels like...it's made of straw. And my special self-made drink is...It helps, but I also don't want to drink too much of it, we haven't got to the hottest part of the day yet. And I'm down to just under half a bottle. And, as much as I like to think this is something I can just keep on producing, I don't know that that's the case. I also find it very difficult to do it... because I can't move my hips or my pelvis or anything. So it's a very awkward task. I tend to fill up my little paracetamol plastic jar that I use and then tip that in, but I do lose half of what I put out...*

I'm sure you're all very interested in this. Well, y'know, what else am I going to talk about? I haven't done much else in the last couple of days, except make a stupid mistake on a rock, and learn how to drink my own piss. And learned that you can eat vanilla Burt's Bees lip balm [eats a bit].

It's not bad.

I'm so thirsty though. I just keep having all these fantasies of fridges full of bottles of, like, fizzy drinks, and cold water, and oh god, no, I can't even think about it, no no no no no no...
Ohhh, man. Never underestimate thirst.

In my unbearable discomfort the pitch of my voice was higher, my words faster, my breathing quickened and swear words more prone to rolling off my tongue. But even in this most dire of moments, through the lens of a camera, in footage that no one might ever see, I still found it almost impossible to cry.

The heat was hurting me, making me utterly desperate. In those moments, enduring the nights no longer seemed painfully slow or unbearably cold. I felt like nothing could be worse than this torture. And the particular thick heat of that Thursday was the most challenging yet. Despite it being late in the day I knew, from the position of the sun, that I had at least another hour of it bearing down on me, of suffering the weight of it. When the temperature hit its peak, the idea of lasting another 24 hours felt so impossible. These were the conditions in which hope most struggled to survive.

If only I could get beneath the overhanging thumb-shaped rock on my right, into the relief of its shadow. If only I could move. I'd made some vain attempts to shuffle my body, using my right arm to tug the band of my shorts, literally trying to yank my body into the shade, while trying to be very gentle, and each time edging millimetre by millimetre closer to the rock. With each pull my body screamed with pain; it felt like a large hot knife stabbing through my side. But I kept trying. Like I said, I was desperate.

One, two, three...YANK.

CHRIST!
I cried out, the pain searing. I wanted to cry.
No. Breathe.
One, two, three...YANK.
Breathe.
A lot of agony for such little recourse. I'd given it as much as I could and had shifted my hips about three inches. If that. I had maybe shaved a minute off my time being under the sun, but then every minute felt like an hour out here. So, despite everything, this still counted for something. I sighed, completely spent. My legs lay like deadweights in the direct heat of the sun. I turned my head towards the overhanging rock, my right hand reaching out towards it, fingertips feeling the mild but sweet relief of its shadow. So close, and yet so far.

The hawks were back. There were two of them now. I watched them circle gently around and around, sweeping a perfect arch high up in the blue above me. A synchronized swim of patience. I wondered whose patience would win out in the end. Theirs or mine.

I've never been a very patient person. I've always wanted things to happen now, and to enjoy things today. Why spend your life preparing when you can spend it living? Then again, what happens when you go out there and live unprepared and everything falls away?

To think that it would all come to end.

Every hope that I ever had would be gone. Just like that. Every memory I held on to for damned dear life would disappear. Every single one of them, erased. All of the things I had learned – the hard way. Growing up, growing older, growing into myself, growing into my own brand of messy realness…I would have gone through it all just to finish up here, in the sand. Gone. The people I knew and loved. The places we'd been together, the things we'd experienced. The memories we had made. It would all be over.

Come on, Nelson.

Don't give up.

You don't want to let all that go.

You're stronger than that.

Aren't you?

High, high above me a tiny white plane moved silently across the sky, cutting a perfect trail of vapour across the vast blue. It was one of several that would pass over during the course of the day, and each time I found myself playing the same game: I wondered where it was headed and thought about the people inside it. Where were they going? Was it excitement or stress that waited for them at the other end? Business or pleasure? Celebration or sadness?

I pictured these travellers. Most of them would be watching movies on their little seat-back screens, or have their faces buried in paperbacks and magazines and laptops. Others would be trying to nap, their seats reclined, jaws slack and eyes scrunched determinedly closed. Perhaps right about now the impeccably dressed flight attendants would be passing through the cabin with their trolley of refreshments, handing out miniature packets of pretzels, holding aloft silver pots of coffee and jugs of water.

Water.

Oh my god, oh my god.

In my mind I heard the snap and hiss of well-manicured fingers cracking open a chilled can of Diet Coke and the image was so tantalizing that it was unbearable. Physically painful. I had started to become obsessed with the idea of Diet Coke, in a can. Always in a can. I wasn't usually a soda drinker but now, here, it was possibly the most glorious-tasting thing I could imagine.

Turning my mind from the refreshments trolley, I pictured someone in a window seat leaning against the smudgy Plexiglass, looking out at the vast, dry desertscape slipping away below them, perhaps daydreaming. I wondered if they might, by some strange defiance of science, be able to see me down here. I imagined how I might look from above – a pale, person-shaped speck laid out in the middle of nowhere, surrounded by boulders. I thought about those chalk drawings cut into a hillside that look like nothing from the ground, but from the air, revealing an arching horse, or the figure of a warrior.

The first day, every time a plane went over, I had waved my hat on the end of my stick in the slimmest of chances that someone might be able to see me and screamed: 'HEY! I'M DOWN HERE!' Of course I knew it was impossible; the plane was so tiny to me, so far above the earth that even if they had a telescope and were actively trying to seek me out, I was far too tiny and hidden in this tiny hole among the shifting shapes and shadows of the vast desert. I was a miniature Jonah and the landscape was the whale that had swallowed me, whole and living, into its belly. Nobody would see me in here.

As time went on, I stopped waving and just watched, helplessly as the planes passed over. And soon enough, each one would disappear. The vapour trail swelled and softened and eventually dissolved into the endless blue. And once again, I was completely alone.

CANADA

I'd been in Canada a month by now, the last two weeks spent mostly on the road, following the general direction of the Trans-Canada highway but unhurriedly shifting through back roads and small towns as I made my way eastward of Montreal.

By the time I got to Quebec City, I had lost myself somewhere in time and place. Maybe time had simply frozen – it would be easy to think so as I wandered the old town, listening to the clip-clop of the horses that pulled elaborate carriages along the cobbles of Rue Saint Louis and watching the drivers' top hats wobbling gently as they passed. And I was frozen too – the place was also simply bone-achingly *cold*. The temperature plummeted deeper into the minuses than I had ever been used to, the parks and gardens were buried knee-deep in snow and early morning shadows of doorways and street lamps trapped a thin layer of ice. Along the quaint and quiet Rue de Petit Champlain, men in bright yellow vests kept watch for pedestrians as a colleague stood atop a ladder hoisting a broom and coaxing sheets of ice from the awnings, letting them tumble onto the street below.

It already felt like a long time ago, but my last week in London had also been one of snow. The kind of snow I hadn't seen in all my 13 years of living there – 'the Beast from the East' they were calling it – a heavy blizzard of white that had blanketed the filthy pavements, burying the scattered litter and coating the brickwork and concrete of the council estates in a generous layer of frosting.

My neighbourhood had looked so quaint and pretty, in a way that Tower Hamlets usually wasn't. The noises of the adjacent highway seemed muffled by the weight of it and it had brought a sense of occasion that only seems to come about with a snow day. Standing by the window, my hands wrapped around a mug of coffee, it had seemed some kind of sign. Either this was the city's attempt to freeze time, keep me there in my flat and in my present life...or it was offering me a clean blank canvas to start afresh with. Preservation or regeneration. Perhaps it was both. The night that I made up my mind to move to Canada I'd looked up visas online and discovered, to my surprise, that I was eligible. New Zealanders could apply up until the grand old age of 35, which was generously later than the cut-off for other nationalities, but at 34, it meant if I was going to do this, I had to do it now. So, I applied right there and then, the light of my laptop screen cutting through the dark. I also knew if I seriously was to explore Canada I would need to finish getting my driver's licence.

When I received confirmation of my Canadian visa the same day I passed my driving test, I took it as a sign that I was going in the right direction.

And then the magazine had shut down. I suppose deep down we all knew it was coming, but without the reliable comfort of my role among the team and the stacks of copy I knew how to juggle I felt more adrift than ever. And more determined of my plans. Certainly everything in my life was ushering me towards the door. There was nothing holding me here now.

At this point in my life London had been the place I felt I most belonged. In many ways it was my greatest romance, and I felt more connected to this rambling, timeworn city than anywhere else, had spent all those years creating a home and a life there. It hurt to realize that the life I had built here was just a temporary installation, so easy to dismantle. Like I'd tried to put down roots on Teflon.

I wasn't sure if I was leaving London because I'd changed, or because London itself had changed. Evidently we were both significantly altered from what we were more than a decade ago. And change was always to be expected in a place like this; London weighs heavy with a dusty permanence, yet it can shape-shift in the blink of an eye. Buildings go up, others come down, streets are replenished by the tide of gentrification, areas take on different personas, adopt new communities – and yet in spite of all this, London remains London. Its changeability is one of its defining characteristics. Perhaps I wasn't changing with it, or at least not in the ways that I needed to. Evidently, the changes I needed to make were not going to happen here. It was time to figure them out and then make them happen. Somewhere else.

Now, I was here. Quebec. Somewhere else. Another city of cobbles and snow, only everything was clean and new to me, a beautiful blank slate.

I had not expected my depression to show up here.

I was calling it that now. *Depression*. After all, I had the pills to go with it, although they were much easier to swallow than the word itself. Easier to call it anxiety or loneliness – wasn't that what it was, in a way? Whatever shame I felt in being lonely, there was far more in being depressed. It didn't even matter that they were common parts of the same machine; words have power. Language matters. And to say the word 'depression' was to admit to something wholly uncomfortable and frightening. It filled me with a deep emptiness, weighing me down with utter hopelessness and a bleak apathy that crawled beneath my skin. Maybe this made me a functioning depressive – like the 'functioning alcoholic' who still manages to keep their life going on the surface while they self-destruct beneath – and that's why I refused to believe for so long I was one at all.

Whatever this was, it was waiting for me when I got up that morning, looming dark over my bedside, watching me put my coat on, then following me through the snowy lanes, always creeping at my heels.

No. You're not supposed to be here. I left you behind.

I had got up early to get some photos of the famous grand hotel Chateau Frontenac before the hordes of tourists arrived and, while it was a bright, clear day, the temperature was sitting at around –11C. Taking off my gloves to fiddle with my digital camera, even for a moment, left my fingers aching with the cold.

Another reason why I got up early was because getting outside was often the best way to shake off the dark moods. I'd felt this one coming on since yesterday, then realized my period was a day or so away, which I knew from experience would only make matters worse – my hormones being proverbial petrol on a garbage-fire of depression. These are what I had come to call Dark Days. They didn't happen often, but when they did, things got bleak. Very bleak. In the worst moments I would cross the street and not even muster the energy to look for oncoming traffic. I really didn't have the energy to care.

At least if something hits me it will stop this god-awful feeling.

And I didn't know what I was more afraid of: the depression or how much I wanted it gone.

I took refuge in a coffee shop, sitting in the window and

clasping a mug of steamy coffee in a bid to bring my sore fingers back to life. I considered what I'd do for the rest of the day. Ordinarily I'd be excited about exploring a new place, but already my enthusiasm was waning. Enthusiasm for anything. Enthusiasm for this coffee. To be outside. To be awake.

Following close behind the shadow of depression was the anguish of guilt. Guilt that I could feel this way having made it here, to actually be driving around Canada, the very thing I had longed for all those anxious nights in London. I was not supposed to feel unhappy. But my head was not here in the romantic, snowy wonderland of Quebec, it had abandoned me for somewhere darker and I couldn't marry that place to the one I was currently sitting in.

Distraction. I had plenty of photos so I posted some to Instagram, sharing moments from my morning, the places I was seeing and exploring. Pretending, in effect, that these were the only things occupying me at the moment. There was no way I could share the unsociable reality of what I was feeling. The idea of revealing that horrified me. Not because people wouldn't care – people care – but because I was sure they wouldn't know what to do with it. If I didn't understand it, how could they? And the great and terrible affliction of being misunderstood was perhaps my deepest fear. God, imagine if anyone thought I didn't want to be here. I wanted to be here, more than anything. I was damn well over the moon to be here. It's just that something in my synapses wasn't letting me feel it.

It was far easier for everyone if I just put my best face forward – the face I wasn't ashamed of. The one people knew how to respond to. A woman having adventures. It wasn't untrue. I *was* a woman having adventures. It's just that…something inside me wouldn't let me feel good about it. And I was ashamed of myself for it.

That's what I'd get if I shared. Shame.

It would be far better to deal with this myself.

I'm fine.

But you're not fine.

You're just good at filtering it.

It's difficult to remember what it felt like to live before social media, and smartphones, and all of the noise that comes with it. My attention span was a hell of a lot better, that's for sure. My emails were longer. And my photos didn't ask for 'likes'. But what was it like to process my thoughts without all the digital accoutrements? To simply think? And feel? And observe? That's what I wonder about now. And whether it's possible to ever go back.

Communication had become so easy and instantaneous that, in many respects, it had made me lazy. Gone were the days spent sitting in internet cafes along Cricklewood Broadway, tucked in among the grimy pubs and dusty convenience shops, meticulously uploading and captioning all my digital photos on a photo-sharing website to send to friends and family. Then I would write long email missives of my travels and my new life in London. Facebook statuses and photo-sharing had long since put paid to that, and now the whole lot had dwindled down to single designated moments from my life, carefully captioned and curated on an app.

Of course, it's not all bad. Facebook put me in touch with those same friends and family I'd been laboriously emailing, letting me post photos and offer brief updates. I'd thought Facebook was marvellous. It saved me a lot of time and pocket change. Then Twitter came in and I used it to follow writers and editors and other successful figures I looked up to. I could converse with the editor on my favourite magazine at the time and when, months later, I applied for an internship there, she put me through with a recommendation. I could reach out and shake the hand of columnists and authors and musicians I admired. Connect with people I would never otherwise be able to connect with. I found my first freelance jobs through Twitter. Made friends that actually translated to real life. It was the chatroom for the modern age.

Once Instagram came about, I suppose we were already so deep in self-curation that nobody noticed what this was doing to our state of mind. An app for photos! Which you can edit! This was fun. You could take a shot of something mundane at a snappy angle, whack a filter on it and share it as if it were a work of art. It became easy to make life look shinier than it really was. I didn't need to tell everybody what I was doing, where I was going...I could just show them a snapshot.

Eventually, Instagram overtook Facebook as the easiest means of keeping track of what friends and family members were doing. Both of my parents joined Instagram. A way to share the small stuff. The joyful mundane. And it became our lens on each others' lives. Family. Friends. Strangers. All of us sharing only the shiny bits. It's an impressive tool for hiding, and one so easy to get hooked on.

The self-curation became frenetic as time went on. Self-expression was run through filters, measured in 'likes' and rewarded with 'followers'. As you compared your life with those who received more likes, it was easy to start thinking that this meant they were more *liked*. More likeable. More loved. So you hide your fuck-ups. Edit out your ugly side. Filter those flaws. This was serious now. One's profile became a brand. You are your brand and you are in competition with other brands. People were looking. Important people. Keep your head up at all times. Don't let them see you fail. Don't let them see you fall apart.

This was all pure kindling to an insecurity fire, reaching into all of us and finding that sensitive spot, the one that holds those primal needs. The need to be loved. And liked. Accepted. And to be seen. Instant validation.

I barely noticed it happening until I was already adapting to it and trying to keep up with it. My social-media posts were real moments from my real life, but in a way they were dishonest by omission. Only share the pretty parts, right? Why tell everyone that I was feeling lonely and anxious when I could share a photo of an amazing flat white on a snowy day in Quebec? Nobody had to know I was sitting in the coffee shop because I was running away from my own depression. By convincing others I was doing fine – get those likes, get that hit of depleted serotonin – I could start to convince myself.

But something had to give. I had to shake myself out of this. *Put the fucking phone away. There's nothing in it to help you.* *But it makes me feel connected.* *And I don't know how to disconnect from it.*

I realized what I needed was a strong dose of the great outdoors, and quickly.

After a reasonable night's sleep I was feeling a bit more myself. I felt reinvigorated with the excitement of purpose. In the corner of a different cafe I was poring over a map of northern Quebec, in awe of the expanse of it. The whole province was massive. Really, freakishly massive. And all its cities were scattered across the very bottom, like the sunken tea leaves in a pot. Once over the St Lawrence River, the region was a colossal expanse of little more than lakes and mountains, stretching all the way up into the Arctic tundra. And there was one place I had my eye on.

Saguenay.

It sounded like a dream.

The more I read about it, the more I knew this was where I had to go.

'The area is located in a depression in the Canadian shield...'

I laughed out loud.

I, too, am located in a depression.

'The relatively small area where the city is located can be described as an isolated oasis in the middle of the vast remote wilderness of northern Quebec. No roads go north into the wilderness; the last roads to the north end just a short distance from the city.'

Sign me up.

It would be remote, but still only three hours from Quebec City, just far enough away to get into wilder spaces. I was making this trip up as I went along, so why *not* head north? I made a few enquiries for dogsledding – it being so late in the season there was only one operator still running, but they could fit me in. It seemed all signs pointed to Saguenay.

There were moments, on my drive north, when I caught glimpses of the scenes I had dreamed about all those months ago. The road cut through rugged mountains, peaks dipped in snow and forests of frosted pines. I longed for the drive to continue, endless and open. But I had a bed in a wooden guest house in the middle of a frozen nowhere and 40 wolf dogs waiting for me.

The first morning, they serenaded me and I was entranced by the sound of them, singing in unison. Forty *awoooos* all at once. Virginie, the young French assistant, stood at the window with her hands wrapped around a mug of coffee, watching the dogs in the throes of their ethereal howl. Her English was very broken but it was better than my French, and we'd managed to converse in fits and starts. She seemed as entranced by the howling as I was.

'Dog song,' I heard her say.

My day on the sled was a dream. There were three sleds heading out and I had one to myself, with my own team of dogs: three malamute-wolf crosses. I stroked their big, thick, fluffy coats with gloved hands, watching their hot breath puff white clouds in the cold air. Standing astride the sled, I had my left boot planted firmly into the wooden footboards, the right pressing onto the metal bar of the claw brake, feeling the grip, feeling in control.

'I won't let you down,' I whispered to my dog team. 'We've got this.'

The yelps and whimpers from the eager dogs exploded into delighted barks as we set off, blazing through the forest, the dogs an arrow through the woods, up trails and down, so fast and so bumpy. I had to shift my weight constantly to meet the leans and curves of the trail. We crossed a great frozen lake, a breathtaking expanse of pure white, and cut a delicate trail across it, a mere scratch on a sheet of glass. It was hard work, and indeed it was work, for the dogs and for us. I kept my eye on that central line, never letting it slacken, wanting those dogs to have faith in me as I had faith in them. I wondered why it was so easy to create such connections with animals, whereas with people we default to the safety of the disconnect. Aren't we pack animals too?

That afternoon I took a drive up to Saguenay Fjords National Park to round off the afternoon with a hike. The trails were covered in snow, and indeed I couldn't even get the car all the way to the trail head, having to traipse the last 10 minutes of road on foot. I swung my water bottle from two fingers, gazing upwards at the flawless blue sky, listening to the snow crunching under my boots, and felt so ludicrously happy to be there. It was like I had forgotten how to be anxious. I was, I later realized, fully outside of my head.

This. This day. This is what I had come for. It's what I had left everything behind for. And I knew then, that this is what had been missing all this time, why everything was out of balance for me. I needed to find a way to incorporate this into my life if I was ever going to change things.

The great outdoors. Nature.

It was becoming clearer to me that loneliness is less about the external factors and entirely about what's going on within. I had felt more isolated and alone in the middle of a room of people I knew in London than up here on this mountain top in the north of Quebec. What I needed was more purpose and more connection to something...there were connections I still had to make within myself. What that looked like was another question.

All I knew for sure was that being in the outdoors gave me a momentary sense of being unlocked.

The next morning I woke up to the chorus of howls. *Dog song.* I lay in bed, feeling lighter than I had in ages. And I realized that the ongoing daily crackles and pain in my back and wrists were gone. I wasn't waking up in pain any more. It was as if my body had started to release whatever it had been holding on to.

The searing afternoon heat was burning away into a warm evening and finally I felt the relief of the hour when the sun finally moved off my face, after some nine hours of bearing down on me. Now its gaze was hidden behind the thumb-shaped rock, I could think straight again. And my first thought was that I couldn't wait for it to get off my legs, too, although this would take another hour.

The next train of thought involved time-keeping. I wondered what time it was in Morocco right now; I figured Nat and Lou should still be there – or had they already headed on to Scotland? I calculated that, either way, it would be the middle of the night, meaning they would still be unaware of my disappearance. They'd be busy on their travels, less likely to realize I'd been quiet back home. So who knew when they might figure it out: tomorrow? Maybe? Hopefully? I could last another day, surely? I had to last another day.

I have to stay alive long enough for someone to notice I am missing.

This was my mantra of sorts now. Because it was my only way out of here – someone clocking my absence. There was no way that someone would stumble upon me here by chance.

I thought of Alison. And whether she would have texted me by now. If she had, I knew that when she didn't hear back it could go one of two ways:

One: she'd be concerned, and maybe she'd think to ask Nat and Lou if they'd heard from me. And then, maybe again, that would start the ball rolling. It was tenuous at best.

Two: she wouldn't be concerned. And why would she be? We'd only just met, she couldn't yet know whether or not I was reliable. She'd probably think I'd gone off-grid for a couple of days. That I was too busy travelling around having a good time. I would be filed under someone who's flakey. Or just really shit at replying to texts. If it were me, that would've absolutely been my assumption.

Still, I had to hope for the first one. As long as there was the smallest possibility of it, I had hope to cling to.

Of course, even in that case there were still maybes to contend with. Say it was assumed that something's wrong, and I was missing: Alison would then need to work out where I was. The only person whom I'd mentioned my plans to was to Lou, in that throwaway text about the rucksack. Which meant if someone realized I was missing, they would need to talk to Lou, and he would need to recall the message and then the pieces of the puzzle would have to be quickly put together. 'She said she was going to hike the Lost Palms Oasis,' Lou would tell them, and in time someone would locate the car at the trailhead.

And then...they would need to be searching outside of the trail itself to get to me.

It made my stomach twist when I thought about how many by-chance factors needed to come together. It seemed like such a delicate thread to hang my hopes from. But it was my only lifeline, the only means of pulling myself out of here. I had to hold on to it as firmly and as long as I could before it snapped.

I picked at the tiny stones that somehow managed to get embedded in my scalp; they were pesky little fuckers, clinging to sweat and skin, coating the backs of my arms like sprinkles on ice cream. Every time I raised my arms I had to brush them off, sending them scattering everywhere, getting in my eyes.

I was tired. So incredibly tired. The pain that consumed my bones and my skin had spread deep into my insides. My kidneys ached, so parched and overworked, forced to recycle urine over and over again. They seemed to retch and gasp inside my abdomen. There were various scrapes and burns on my skin which rubbed against the stones, and the blistered agony of my heels. The pain, the discomfort, the heat, the unending thirst...I felt so worn out, like I could close my eyes and sleep for ever.

For that reason I dared not sleep during the day, when the heat already threatened to consume me. I had to keep myself awake and aware, to survive, and in case anybody came looking for me.

[video] *Why is it still so hot?...Tonight is so hot...I feel like I'm just burning.... I can't...I really want to take my boots off, I've got blisters on the heels...But I can't reach them. I'm so uncomfortable.* [Slow panting] *When is my...When am I going to be rescued? When is someone gonna come looking for me? ...This tr....* [licks lips] *This heat is trying to get to me.* [Whispers] *I won't let it.*

My mouth had turned to straw, my lips sticking to my gums and my tongue rasping across the insides of my cheeks like chalk on a drywall. The discomfort of it could only be relieved by trickles of urine splashed onto my tongue and swished around in my mouth. Holding my nose eased the vileness of the taste, but the aftertaste that lingered in the back of my nose was harder to eradicate. The meagre solution was to scrape my lip balm across my teeth, pressing it against the inside of my gums with my tongue, coating my mouth with a faint hint of vanilla.

I was becoming seriously worried about the liquid situation. I was down to less than half a bottle. It wasn't the current shortage that worried me so much as the reliability of the source: as much as I liked to think urine was something I could keep on producing, I couldn't know for sure that it was. Every time I collected some in the paracetamol jar I would lose more than half of it – it's hard enough to aim into a small container, but doing so while lying down, unable to move your legs, or sit up, and wracked with the pain of tensing the body, it was a challenge. And a task I had come to detest. Not only that, but as I became more dehydrated I would certainly produce less liquid and what I did produce would become more concentrated, more toxic. I had no way of being sure when that stage had been reached.

So urine was a quick fix; a balm. It was not going to sustain me indefinitely. In my head I was constantly thinking of 'input' vs 'output'. The word 'INFRUITION' running down the side of the clear plastic bottle was my measuring guide: I had to keep the level above the final 'i' at all times. That was my comfort point, my goalpost; keeping it above that level was my greatest task. Because once I'd run out of drinkable pee, that would be it.

I continued having fantasies about water. Those fridges full of dewy, glass bottles. So painful and visceral that I would have to scold myself, out loud, to snap out of it.

NO. STOP IT.

I wasn't hungry. Hunger felt like an entirely fictional concept to me now. What was that like? How strange it was to have forgotten the very notion of eating. In London, my life had revolved so gratuitously around food; my peers and I were always seeking out the latest restaurant, bakery, taqueria, noodle bar…it was not just the sphere in which my professional life orbited, it had become my world. Even when I travelled, it was often focused around that simple and effusive question: where should we eat?

Food filled the void of everything else. The experience of eating had become my social crutch. I had my food friends, with whom I'd meet up just to check out some pop-up diner, or supper-club, or hot new hole-in-the-wall. Sometimes the only excuse I found to get myself out of the house was to venture out to a coffee bar or favourite snack spot – Fabrique bakery for sticky, Scandi-style cinnamon buns, or St John for a plump donut filled to bursting with vanilla-bean custard. London does food well, and the scene never rests for even a moment. New restaurants bloomed like flowers in a garden, and for every one that died off, several more seemed to take its spot. There was always somewhere new to stuff your face. And for me, it was part of the job. Consuming fine foods and wine at a chef-packed event had become as normal to me as Friday night takeout. Mine had become a gluttonous life, and I'd adored the constant comfort and curiosity that came with it.

Now, though, I was surprised to find I couldn't remember what hunger felt like. What it was to crave food. The very notion of it had become meaningless. My body had shut off my appetite like an electrician turning off the mains power, cravings and fancies shut down, taste's sensory synapses still, everything faded to black.

In the back of my mind I knew I should try to keep myself sustained. That somehow I should get food into my body. My bagel had remained largely untouched in my lunch bag, softening slowly in the heat to the point that the filling and the bread had become indistinguishable from one another, a sort of avocado-bread mush. Using my dry, cardboard mouth to bite and chew was no longer an option, so I tried pinching off a piece of bagel mush, rolling it between my forefinger and thumb, and, like a pill, placing it on the sandpaper surface of my tongue.

Go on. Eat. Keep your strength up.

And just like a pill, the piece of food clung to the side of my throat. I coughed. It wouldn't go down, and simply tumbled around in my dry mouth like a tiny cork. There was no saliva, no moisture, to carry it.

I spat it out.

I was too dried up.

I didn't want to eat anyway.

The human body can go without food for ten days. But it was what...three days that you can go without water? I wondered whether that duration might be even shorter in the desert. At best, I was nearing my limit. At worst...

The CamelBak reservoir had long since been sucked dry; all that remained of my water were two drops, clinging to the thick blue polyurethane. I pressed my thumb against them, saw the water drops spread out then reform the moment I let go, dancing a little ballet. Try as I might, I could not get them out. They stuck there. God, I wanted them. I imagined how they would feel on my tongue, absorbed into the surface – melted ice cream on hot beach sand. But how sweet those drops would taste.

I had a greater longing for those two drops of water than I'd ever had for the most delectable fancies in the world of gourmet cuisine. Water. It was the divine.

Sucking with all my force on the drinking tube drew them close to the small valve, but no further. I yanked off the piping and tried to coax the drops through the main opening in the bag, even shaking the opening over my mouth, but they clung to the plastic, refusing to come out. I was desperate. Obsessed. I wanted nothing more in the world than to get to those drops of water. Pressing my thumbs against the outside of the CamelBak I slowly coaxed them, a few millimetres at a time, to the other end, closer to the opening. I took off the screw-cap and tried to hook them out – first with my finger, then with my tongue, swiping at the inside of the CamelBak, tasting only hot plastic. Bone dry.

By this point I was ready to tear the plastic with my teeth and get to those droplets. That was the only way left, surely. It would be hard to tear it, but do-able. First, though, I had one more idea. I screwed the lid back on, put my lips over the hose attachment and began to blow into it, inflating it like a balloon at a birthday party. I wondered, if I left this out in the sun, in this almighty heat, might condensation eventually form? Might this mean more drops? More liquid to quench my tongue?

I know. This was reaching. Implausible, probably. Science was never my forte and I didn't have the know-how to be sure this would even work. I was merely recalling the many times I'd woken up in a tent in full sunlight, the polyester lining coated in a dew from the heat of breath. So maybe it was a stupid idea, but nothing could be more stupid than not trying at all.

In the meantime, I considered the rest of my gear: what else might conceivably pass for liquid sustenance? My right hand rummaged through the contents of my kit bag: sunscreen? No. Hand sanitizer – definitely not.

Urine. Fucking urine. That was all I had.

[video] *I hate trying to collect urine, I hate drinking urine, I hate the fact I'm shouting and shouting for hours, for three days now, and there's no one around to listen. There's no other walkers out here, no one's come looking for me…I have to assume no one's sent a search party out which means no one's noticed that I haven't been home. I'm really trying not to give up hope. Really trying. I can hear lots of planes going over – none of them are planes that are looking for anybody…I don't know how long I can go on living off my own urine, you know?*

––––––––––––––

It was dusk, the sky now shaking away the last embers of sunlight, turning everything a dark grey and heading into black. Another night. My third. I dreaded it as much as ever, the long, slow crawl into darkness, the biting cold, the hours of black uncertainty, the not knowing what was out there and what might find its way to me. Quietly waiting out the night for a new day, new hope. I prayed that I would sleep through most of it, that unconsciousness would shorten the time spent feeling frozen with both cold and fear. Dawn could never come quickly enough.

The desert seemed so still that evening; an otherworldly sense of calm hung thick and still in the air. The rocks around me seemed to hum faintly with an unfamiliar energy. There was a strangeness and a peace about the place that I hadn't felt before now.

It had been a damn good ride, this life. I got to do all of this, I got to be here, for the finite time I had been given. And I had followed my heart, many times. It had taken me to some weird and wonderful places. It was my heart that had led me here. To this canyon. Was there not some comfort to be found in that?

A sudden movement distracted me from my reverie. I raised my eyes to the rocks that loomed high above me. There was something there, up in the boulders. Something moving in the darkness.

Snakes?

Please not snakes.

The strangeness of this night, the stillness, gave the possibility of snakes a particular potency. Just my luck that tonight they would come out.

I caught the flicker of movement again. And then I saw what it was.

There were little bats flitting among the rocks high above me. I glimpsed them as they moved out from the shadows, points of ears and the flutterings of wings, origami darts against the deep blue-grey sky. They were going about their business, either unaware of my presence or entirely disinterested. Perhaps they had realized I was not a threat to them. Were they a threat to me? My instincts swiftly moved through fear and uncertainty and settled into acceptance and wonder, and as my eyes became accustomed I watched the bats with curiosity as they went about their nightly forage. I felt an overriding feeling of peace wash over me. The bats were not menacing, but mesmerizing. How beautiful, I thought. How strange I am only seeing them tonight.

How strange this night feels. How peaceful.

Is this what it feels like when you're going to die?

Is this how it ends?

I was sinking into acceptance, I think. I simply didn't have the energy to fight the inevitable any more. But something was shifting. Something only just perceptible. A creeping sensation of calm, of presence and of place – of seeing things not as a spectator but as if I was now one with the scenery. Becoming absorbed into the earth, forming a part of the landscape, existing for the time I had left among the cacti and the creosote, the dirt and rocks and the creatures that hid themselves within it all. The secret life of the desert carried on around me, unthreatened and unafraid. In a strange way, I felt lucky to be here to witness these things in my last moments. And I realized that if this really was where I died, out among the wild things, it would not be the worst place. In fact, of all the locations where my bones could rest, I would be happy that this was mine.

As I closed my eyes again I felt fear leave me and, in its place, only gratitude.

A bright light played against my eyelids.

Light?

Where was it coming from?

I opened my eyes. Above me hung the moon, a dazzling white globe, a spotlight that seemed to be trained directly into the clearing in which I lay. Everything was lit up – the boulders in highlight, shadows pooling behind them, the gritty sand on which I was lying sharpened into detail. The desert, bathed in this ethereal glow, was so impossibly still that for a moment I wondered whether I had entered into a dream. Another realm. An afterlife of sorts.

I tried to shift my body. No. I was still here, still breathing, still in pain. It was just me and the moon, gazing at one another. And then a thought: might there be coyotes tonight? Under a moon like this? Surely, tonight of all nights, I would hear them.

Maybe this calm is the moment before I die.

And then a scratching sound, coming from somewhere very close behind my head.

I was not the only one awake in the moonlight.

A cold fear ran through my blood. There really was something there.

This was it. This was the end, wasn't it?

Wasn't it?

The rustling moved from my right to my left, still somewhere behind my head, and my body turned to stone. My eyeballs were now the only thing moving, rolling up in their sockets to try and see what had entered my enclosure. And it wasn't long before I caught a glimpse out of the corner of my eye.

A mouse. So tiny, I could have enclosed it in my hand. Clearly I had been lying here so still and for so long that my presence was no longer a concern to bats or to mice. I sighed gently, relieved and amused, my breath making a faint cloud in the cold night air.

Hey, little buddy.

This time I only thought the words, not daring to speak out loud, not even sure if I could any more...I just lay there and watched in fascination as life around me carried on.

The mouse moved in small, darting starts and stops, checking side to side every few steps, all the while making a determined beeline towards my trash container. On top of the container my bagel perched, still in its wrapping but long since discarded. The fact I had not bothered to put it back inside the container was a sign that my motivation was running on a low ebb. I'd got tired and lazy. The mouse certainly seemed to know precisely where it was going; I wondered when it had clocked the food source and whether it had been waiting to make certain that I wasn't dangerous. I wondered how long it had waited.

I even, for a moment, wondered if this was my mind playing tricks on me again. That I had hallucinated a mouse. But no...it was definitely here.

Its little teeth pulled at the loose wrapping of the bagel – tug tug tug – and sent it tumbling gently, wrapping and all, onto the sand. It was at this point that a second mouse appeared from around a rock. I watched, wide-eyed, mesmerized, as the two little creatures worked together to claim the bagel, dragging it around the rock and out of sight.

Well, I'm glad it didn't go to waste.

And then I laughed – a raspy, breathy chuckle, bewildered that I could still find amusement out here.

All was not lost. Yet.

Day Four:
Friday

I woke up. Still alive. I had survived a third night, but the agonizing discomfort that wracked my body seem to be reaching new peaks. My bones felt hot, like they were burning me inside my skin, which was itself getting burned, red patches throbbing across my arms, belly, legs. And I had been in the same position all this time; not being able to roll on to my side and take the strain off my back was a torture on its own.

At least during the night I had managed to fill my bottle of 'special drink' to over the halfway mark, which was a small win. And to my mind, it meant I should still be able to survive the day. In terms of faux-hydration, anyway.

The camera was low on battery and whined as I turned it on. Like me, it was still going, but just barely. I recorded another message, trying to express some dregs of hope to myself and to anyone who might see it. But my voice was growing weaker, my throat raspy. It was short. And signed off with the thing I couldn't say enough.

I love you all so much.

To watch that video now, I'm horrified at how sunken my face was after just three days. My lips clung to my gums like Velcro making my teeth seem horselike and huge, while my eyes were narrow, creased pockets.

I was about to say something else, to add a little note of optimism, when the camera whirred, the lens clacking for a moment then whining sadly as it retracted for the last time. The battery had finally run out. There were no resources left for optimism.

I hadn't realized it until that moment but having the camera had given me something. Something I'd been holding on to: a feeling that I wasn't totally disconnected, that I wasn't completely alone and that – somehow – the situation wasn't entirely hopeless. What it had given me was another strand of hope, and I hadn't truly understood how much of it had been wrapped up in that little camera. In a way, the eye of the lens had made me feel like I was seen. It had given me a voice, as my journal once did. In that same way it let me share my hopes and fears. My experiences and my plans. Through it, I felt I could still speak to others, to reach out and touch them, and keep a connection going to the world so it wouldn't keep turning without me.

There is something to be said for having somebody to talk to.

The first time I watched that scene in *Castaway*, when Wilson the volleyball floats out to sea and Tom Hanks shouts after him, distraught, I'd felt sad, but I took it rather lightly. (Who hasn't reenacted that scene on the edge of a beach?) Now, it doesn't seem comical. I get it. I really *get it* now. And I wonder if Tom Hanks's character would have survived as long as he did if he hadn't had Wilson. A volleyball for a companion is far better than no companion at all. When I think of that scene I feel the agonizing pain of isolation, the despair of losing that last connection with another person, real or not. The need for connection, the need to be seen, is what makes us human.

This is surely why we take to social media so wholeheartedly. In the absence of company, one can usually find some kind of method of conversation, and by its very nature, the internet gives us a social substitute, a virtual interaction. Social media lets us join the masses in the ether. It gives us an outlet for thoughts. And I'd gotten so used to that I suppose. All those times I'd felt enveloped in solitude, I'd at least had social media to fill the gap. I could reach out and prod the rest of the world and let them know: I'm here. But I fooled myself into thinking of that as connection, distracting myself from the painful process of opening up and making concrete ones in real life.

Out here in the desert, the camera was the closest thing I had to fill any of those gaps and I hadn't even realized what it had meant to me. Venting into the black glassy iris of a retractable lens to everybody and anybody and nobody all at once gave me a voice. A way to be heard. To be seen. And maybe, if I was very lucky, to be understood.

If I had felt alone these past days, with just a camera for company, it was nothing to how I felt now. With the camera dead, it was just me and the cripplingly vast expanse of the desert, my body invisible and my absence unnoticed.

I had never felt lonelier than this.

By the afternoon I was drifting in and out.

Semi-conscious.

Weakening.

Sounds muffled.

Senses softened.

Woozy.

I wasn't always sure when I was asleep and when I was awake.

I was running. Bare feet across hot sand. Little red shorts with the piping on the edges. The sound of cicadas. A hot day. A sticky New Zealand summer. Such a hot day. So hot. I was thirsty. I wanted

*some juice. There was juice in the fridge. Dad? Mum? I was running.
The cry of seagulls. The song of the ice-cream van jangling in the
next street over. Chris? Bare feet on hot sand. Look out for shells. So
thirsty. Someone was shouting. Who? Where was my big brother?
Had something happened again? Bare feet on hot sand. So hot. I
was running. I wiped my sweaty hands on my shorts. It was hot. The
smell of the sea. The jingle of the ice-cream van. I wanted juice. I was
running. So hot. So thirsty. Where was everybody? Anybody? Bare
feet on hot sand. I had to get to the fridge. I was running. Bare feet
on hot concrete. So thirsty. I needed juice. But someone was shouting
something...*

'FUCKIN' COYOTE!'

I opened my eyes.

That was a voice. It had been so clear, it could have been
somebody sitting right there in the canyon with me. But obviously
there was no one here.

Had that been a part of my dream, or was it real?

No. Someone had definitely shouted. Something about a
coyote. Someone close by. My head was woozy from the heat and
the daze of coming to. What was the voice? Was there someone
here? Was there a coyote here?

My heart raced as I strained to hear something.

A sound.

Anything.

Wait.

I heard something.

It was very distant.

It was the beating of a helicopter.

My breath stopped tight in my chest as I listened for more,

not daring to believe that this was real. After all, I had thought I'd heard a helicopter yesterday. This might be all in my head. I'd probably gone fully fledged mad.

Then that same voice came again, as if out of the sky, as clear as a bell.

'...WE'RE SEARCHING FOR A MISSING HIKER.'

There are moments in life that you will never forget. That are seared in your brain like the light through a pinhole camera, capturing something perfectly permanent. And these words hit me like a welcome sucker punch, like a violently exuberant embrace from someone you haven't seen in far too long. My instinct was to scramble to my feet, to jump up and down waving my arms and screaming, 'HEY! I'M HERE!'

Of course, I couldn't do that.

My brain raced to put my options together. And I wondered, could it be me they were looking for? Who was this missing hiker? Was this a search party for someone else? Or was it me? Either way, this was my only chance to get out. They were looking! They had to see me!

It was impossible to tell where the helicopter actually was; all I could see was the same unmoving circle of boulders, and beyond that the same empty blue sky, while the beating of the blades seemed to drift into the canyon on the breeze from all directions.

But I didn't need to see them – I just needed them to see me. I screamed as hard as my lungs could handle: 'I'M HERE! HELP MEEEEE! PLEASE!'

I picked up the end of the hiking stick and waved my sun shade as hard as I could, the tattered white plastic bag that flapped on the end looking like a white flag of surrender, waving at nobody in particular. Waving at the sky.

I listened for a response, heart in my mouth, but all I could hear was the distant whir of the helicopter. It was growing fainter. It was going further and further away. The helicopter was leaving.

'NO! PLEASE! COME BACK! I'M HERE! I'M DOWN HERE!'

By the time my echoes had dissolved into the boulders, there was no sound of the helicopter any more.

It was gone.

OK, Nelson. Don't panic. They're looking for a hiker. This is good. This is very good.

They'll have to come back. They have to. They were looking.

They have to come back.

My heart raced, adrenaline fizzing through me, as I considered all options that were open to me now. I needed them to return to the canyon, to fly over this hole so they could spot me.

Please come back. Please come back.

Please.

It was difficult to know how much time passed. It felt like 20 minutes; it could have been five.

And then...I heard it. Yes! The beating of the helicopter.

They had come back.

Thank you, thank you, thank you.

Again, I couldn't see it, but I heard that same voice come out of the sky again, a man's voice, clear as a bell.

'CLAIRE NELSON. WE'RE LOOKING FOR YOU.'

Oh my god...

'IF YOU CAN, MAKE ANY SIGNAL SO WE CAN SEE YOU...'

I waved the sun shade so vigorously that the movement yanked painfully at my broken bones, but I didn't stop.

'I'M HERE! I'M DOWN HERE! I'M HERE! PLEASE!'

For a split second I saw the chopper, passing behind the distant clifftop to my left. A flash of black and white, visible for a moment and then it was gone. But I continued waving and screaming, knowing that as long as I could hear the helicopter blades, I had a chance.

The voice asked again for a signal.

I had tried so hard to be visible but they couldn't see me down here. I had no other way to get their attention other than what I was currently doing. Unless they flew directly over me, I was shit out of luck.

'I'M HERE! I'M DOWN HEEEEERE!'

But the sound of the blades began to grow fainter again as the helicopter turned away and, once more, the canyon was returned to silence.

My heart sank into my gut, feeling an aching terror as I realized how close I had come to getting out of this place, how utterly, painfully near they had been. I had seen the helicopter. I had seen them and they had not seen me. I had missed my chance. I felt completely spent, drained and heavy with despair.

Please come back. Please come back.

Please. Please. Please.

But I knew, even if they ever came back, the same thing would happen over and over. I'd scream and wave and they wouldn't be able to see me. Maybe there were people on foot out searching as well. Maybe they'd have more luck finding me. If they came down this far off the trail...And searching on foot would take a lot longer. How much longer was anyone's guess.

I had to make myself more visible to the search helicopter. I yanked the white Stater Bros bag from the sun shade, feeling the heat bearing down on me, and set about some reinforcements. I hung my Bob Dylan t-shirt over the cross of the sun shade like a scarecrow. I stretched the tattered white plastic bag across it again, securing it at the arms, making it as big and as white as I could, and hung my straw hat on the very top. My flag was now larger. Still pathetically insufficient, but it was all I had.

Who knows how much time passed after that. Time had lost all shape to me now.

Forty minutes? Fifteen minutes? Two?

I felt like I was holding my breath.

And I prayed. Prayed at the altar of this earth, whatever powers that be, prayed to the Universe, flat on my back but, in my mind, on my knees and begging for mercy.

Please. Let them come back. Let them come back and let them see me. This is it. This is my only chance. I want to keep living, I want to do it better, and I will do it better, just let them come back.

Please, let them see me.

Then the sound.

That glorious sound.

The helicopter had returned.

One more time.

I was ready. I was about to give this everything I had, I just had to hope they came close enough to see my movements. I held the hiking stick by the very tip, with just my fingertips and, stretching my arms up into the sky, I held my makeshift flag as high as I could without dropping it. I waved it furiously, back and forth, back and forth, my Bob Dylan T-shirt dancing in the late afternoon sunlight. *Listen to that Duquesne whistle blowing.*

I don't even know why I bothered to scream, given they would not have been able to hear me. But I screamed again and again: 'I'M DOWN HERE! PLEASE! PLEASE! I AM HERE!'

Then that voice came again.

This time, with the words I will never, ever forget.

'CLAIRE, WE SEE YOU...WE'RE GOING TO COME AND GET YOU.'

The world spun like a top.

The hiking stick clattered to the sand beside me as I let my arms fall, spent and rested on the earth, their work done, and I sobbed under the weight of the relief that rained down on me...washing over me, my emotions rolling over and over like a wave and flooding me with a single realization:

I am going to live.

I could let go now. I could finally let go. It was no longer down to me alone to get myself out of here, and I could hand over the controls. Someone else was driving.

They were going to come and get me.

And I was going to live.

I eagerly prepared myself for rescue, hastily stuffing my t-shirt, camera and anything else salvageable into the rucksack. I lay there clutching my stick, ready to go, like a kid waiting to be picked up after sports practice. I was shaking.

I waited.

It must have been almost an hour later when I heard men's voices coming from somewhere above me, and the heavy tread of booted footsteps. The presence of other people out here made me giddy. I couldn't get a handle on my emotions: I wanted to laugh, to sing, to leap right up and throw a hug at whoever these people were.

'Claire?'

'Yes!' I rasped, 'I'm down here!'

'OK, we're coming down!'

I heard scuffling boots and a murmur of conversation. More scuffling, the sound of rocks rolling and dirt scattering. A pause.

'How the hell did you get down there?' one of them shouted.

'The hard way!' I shouted back.

Christ, I was ridiculously fucking happy. I had never felt as happy as I did at that moment.

Found. I'd been found. Elation had kicked in, hard.

The boot steps grew closer, and then more scrambling as one and then two men in khaki jumpsuits and sunglasses clambered into view.

'Boy, am I glad to see you guys,' I said, amusing myself with the cliché. I almost giggled.

There was some tricky footwork to be done and the two rescuers took a little time helping one another make their way down to me without injuring themselves in the process. One of them dropped his radio, sending it sliding and clattering onto rocks. Some cursing. I grimaced, feeling bad for the trouble I was putting these guys to.

'Did you bring your radio?' he called to his partner, 'I think mine's broken.'

It really wasn't an easy place to get to. Nobody would have found me here by chance. Also, I really hoped like hell they had another radio, or else we wouldn't be going anywhere anytime soon.

But after a bit of legwork, there they were, two officers standing over me, assessing the scene, taking in the sight of this crumpled hiker they'd been looking for.

Man, they looked so tall.

'Apologies...' I said, 'I smell pretty bad.'

They both laughed and shook their heads. 'Oh believe me, we've smelled SO much worse.'

Manny and Eric were deputies for the Riverside Sheriff Aviation Unit. Eric had been piloting the helicopter while Manny was on lookout. How they found me was actually a chain of tiny miracles. Of course, I didn't know any of this at the time. All I knew was that they were my knights in khaki armour.

'Can you move?'

'No. I've shattered my pelvis. I can't even sit up.'

'How long have you been out here?'

'Since Tuesday.'

'Jesus.'

The two discussed the best plan of action.

'We were thinking we might be able to carry you out, but

from the looks of your injuries there's no way we wanna move you. We're going to have to radio for some assistance. We'll get someone out here as quickly as we can, OK?'

'Sure, I'm not going anywhere.'

From inside the rocky canyon not even the police radios could pick up any signal, so Manny clambered out into the clearing and awkwardly made his way back up to higher ground to get a radio signal and call for back-up. I didn't know what was going on but much later I understood it was the California Highway Patrol unit who took the call.

'OK,' he said, picking his way back down to the clearing. 'We've got a stretcher coming with another chopper, so we can lift you out.'

'How long till they get here?'

'Hard to say, it depends where their unit is, but I'd say about an hour.'

In the meantime, we would wait.

Several small bottles of water were produced and one was handed to me.

Oh my god.

I had water.

In all my life, through all those years of professional gluttony and culinary travels, nothing had ever seemed as divinely decadent as that single bottle of water.

I don't even remember what that first sip tasted like. In truth I drank it so fast, it long since becoming a need rather than a want, letting it fill my mouth, and gulping it the way a drowning man takes his first breath on the surface. The water barely made contact before disappearing, like it was poured on to scorched earth.

Another two bottles were placed beside me. The sight of them made me feel soothed and safe. My days of dehydration were over. I would not ever have to suffer the pain of it again, to feel that agonizing longing. There was water here.

'Are you hungry?' asked Eric.

'Not at all.'

'I have an apple if you want one?'

And suddenly he produced one from his pocket, holding it up to the light. A shiny, juicy red apple. It practically sparkled. Suddenly, it was all I had ever wanted.

I devoured it right down to the pips.

The two deputies perched on the boulders within my rocky den, either side of me, each trying to stay in the shade as best they could to avoid the sun. Having other people suddenly taking up the space in my enclosure of rock felt so strange. But wonderfully so.

I cracked open the second bottle of water, which, despite my better instincts, I immediately began to guzzle.

'Take it slowly, OK?'

And, while we waited for back-up, we just chatted. Shooting the breeze, getting to know each other, as if we were sitting at the pub nursing pints of ale – not in a desert valley, clutching plastic bottles of water, with one of us lying on their back in their own stench. I don't think any of us could quite make sense of it.

'This is so crazy,' said Manny. 'I can't wait to tell the guys about this!'

I told them my story: the hike, the fall, the dehydration, drinking urine, the desperate cravings I'd had for Diet Coke, the mice that had come in the night and taken my bagel...Having someone to talk to was almost as delicious as the apple.

In return, the officers told me about the call-out. How they'd been informed I'd been missing – the details being that I was likely gone Tuesday and possibly while walking the Lost Palms Oasis trail.

'In this heat, after that many days, we kind of figured we might be looking for a body,' said Manny.

They'd been searching for me on the trails, picking over the miles and miles of low desert valley, cliffs and boulders and rocky tundra, endless brown earth. And they'd seen nothing. Eric then recalled an area a little further south where someone had gone missing about a decade before. They decided they should at least fly over and check it out. When that search yielded nothing, they had to start making their way back to base, low on fuel and needing to regroup. And it was that route out of the park that brought them over this area where Manny spotted something moving: a quick glimpse of a tiny white speck in the sea of desert below. It looked like a common piece of trash blowing around in the valley – 'There's a lot of that about,' he said. But something stood out. 'Wait. Go back.' He grabbed the binoculars and had Eric circle back. Just to check. Just to be absolutely sure. Which is when he caught a glimpse again: that movement.

That's not trash. That's the hiker.

They had seen me.

'We have a wall in our unit of pictures of the people we find alive – most of the time what we find isn't good, so it helps to keep us going, y'know? So sometime, if you were OK with it, we'd love to get a photo with you for the wall.'

'Of course! But...not right now. I mean, this is not exactly profile-picture material.'

The guys roared.

'I can't believe you've been out here four days and you're making jokes!'

'You don't understand,' I said, craning my head and grinning, 'this is the happiest day of my life!'

Manny helped me crack the third bottle of water. This time I remembered to sip it.

And then I remembered something I'd wanted to ask.

'The first thing I heard was something about a coyote...'

The two deputies looked at one another like they'd been busted.

'Man, I told you!' said Eric, pointing an accusatory finger at Manny.

'We were looking for you and I saw some hikers on the trail,' said Manny, as Eric rolled with mirth. 'And I saw an animal coming towards them, so I told them to take another direction...'

'Yeah, and then you turned to me and said...'

'I said: "it's a fucking coyote!"'

'Yeah, you said "it's a fucking coyote"! To the whole damn desert! He kept telling me I still had my foot on the mic pedal,' said Manny, 'But I was sure I didn't say it over the speaker.'

I grinned. 'You did.'

And we all laughed. The three of us, having a laugh in the weirdest possible hangout under the weirdest possible circumstances. My god, I never thought I'd have a laugh with other people ever again and now, here we were.

Within an hour, another helicopter appeared over the valley, the California Highway Patrol. Manny told me they'd have some pain meds for me.

'CHP's here. Close your eyes, it's about to get windy!'

I felt the coarse sand and dirt begin to pick up and whip at my skin as the chopper closed in overhead. A large bag was sent down – supplies – followed by a flight officer in a sand-coloured jumpsuit, who zipped down on a long-line, landing in a nearby clearing. Mere moments later, there were four of us in the little canyon.

I couldn't see her face clearly beneath the flight helmet, but I learned her name was Jen. And she was about to say words I didn't want to hear.

'We're going to roll you on to the stretcher, OK?'

Wooooooah, no no no.

There was no way that could happen. For me to be lifted I was going to need some serious pain medication. To even *contemplate* it.

'Painkillers...' I croaked, struggling to get the words out. Since I'd started drinking water my tongue had begun to swell like a sponge, giving me a lisp. And then, more words I didn't want to hear.

'We don't have any medication here. But we're going to take you for treatment right now.'

The CHP was essentially the evacuation team, and they had nothing to give me for the pain. Not so much as an aspirin. And I found myself suddenly torn: I wanted to get out of here, but not like that.

Anything but that.

'We're going to need to roll you, just enough to get the stretcher under you.'

'No no...I can't, I really can't...'

'It's the only way we can get you out of here. The sooner we can get you out of here the sooner we can get you something for the pain, OK?'

My head shifted in a small nod, my heart hammering. I wanted to get out of here more than anything, but the idea of how painful this was going to be made me shake. *Pain or death,* I reminded myself. Maybe I could let pain win this one. After all, this time I had back-up.

Think of the hospital bed.

Think of the water.

Think of the pain meds.

As instructed, I folded my arms across my chest. Then squeezed my eyes shut and clenched my teeth. Manny at my shattered hip, Jen beside him, ready with the stretcher, Eric on my right.

'One, two, three—'

Manny would later tell me how he felt and heard the shards of my bones crackling inside my pelvis as he lifted me. All I remember is a blinding flash of white, the most horrific, searing pain of my life so far, and that I grabbed Eric's shoulder so hard I thought I could have ripped it from its socket. I let out a guttural scream from somewhere so deep within me that, I would find out later, made no sound at all. A silent scream for mercy.

'You didn't pass out, though,' Jen would tell me when we met again, months later. 'Which I had thought you might.'

Now that the stretcher was underneath me, they had to lower me back on to it, and by this stage I was a whimpering wreck. But I was so ready to leave this place.

The stretcher bumped and jolted as the crew worked to slip it into a bag – a body bag, I couldn't help thinking – and zipped it all the way, leaving just a little gap for my mouth and nose. I squinted against the sand being whipped about, caught a hazy glimpse of khaki uniform before I closed my eyes entirely and felt myself carried to the nearest clearing, my body in agony. Then, a tug at my belly as I was plucked from the earth and lifted, suddenly weightless, swaying gently beneath the thumping heartbeat of the helicopter, my eyes shut tight against the churning wind and sand, unable to see much but my mind's eye picturing the canyon falling away beneath me. The canyon. The place I had really thought was going to be my final resting place.

I was free.

Recovery

PALM SPRINGS

It's hard to remember the order of things now. Moments float among one another in my memory as tiny snapshots. Lying flat on my back on a gurney in the intensive-care unit. Dim lighting. Every whip of the curtain at my feet revealing the corridor, with its flurry of people passing to and fro. Machines. Beeps. Alarms. Different faces coming in. Someone delivering my bag and hiking stick, recovered from the two deputies. The cheery attendants from Mercy Air, wearing their white coveralls, coming to check on me and delivering a small helicopter pin – 'a souvenir of your flight...if you want to remember it!' I did remember it: the CHP helicopter lowering me on to tarmac (Chiriaco Summit airport, I later learned), the bag unzipped and the sun so bright that the crew of people gathered around me were nothing more than silhouettes. Someone held my hand and offered me reassurance as I was hooked up to equipment.

'*Painkillers?*'

'Sure thing, sweetheart, we're getting you some morphine right now.'

I barely noticed the first dose enter my system. I was lifted one more, into the Mercy Air heli-ambulance. Space was tight, the interior a cramped, white box of machines. A headset was placed over my ears so I could communicate amid the din of helicopter noise and radio crackles. My voice pleading, my swollen tongue begging for more morphine and the promises that there would be more soon.

'Once we get to the hospital.'

'How long?'

'I'd say about 20 minutes.'

I remembered the journey, although I never actually saw the helicopter pin, which in an instant became lost in the detritus of the hospital.

I can remember the nurse easing my beloved boots off my blistered feet, to be bagged up for safe-keeping, and the gush of relief I felt at having my feet freed at last. How strange and wonderful it felt. A cool, crisp sheet was draped over me for privacy as my clothes were sliced off with a pair of scissors, my broken body released from filthy fabric piece by piece, each one tossed into a biohazard bin. A soft, clean blue gown was tucked around my scuffed and broken body. Wires taped to my chest. Then the beaming face of an orderly ducked through the curtain with a gift.

'I heard you were looking for one of these?' as he held up a can of Diet Coke.

'How did you...'

'We all know about you,' he said, waving away my surprise. 'You're a bit of a celebrity round here! You're a survivor.'

The deputies must have mentioned it and word passed down. I was confused. Humbled. Overwhelmed by the kindness. Baffled as to why strangers would know about me. Taken aback that I had a can of Diet Coke, for so long taunting me between conscious and subconscious, and now right here, at my bedside. For once in my life I didn't have the capacity to squirm about kindness being offered to me – instead I welcomed it in, and realized how good it felt to do so. I gazed at the can with stupefied awe.

'Can I drink it?'

'Not yet, honey,' said a nurse. 'We're waiting on the doctor before you can have a drink.'

All of this was happening to me and around me, while my mind floated somewhere above it all, elated and in disbelief.

And then, someone handed me a cordless telephone.

'It's your mother.'

My mother? Her sudden presence in this American hospital unit came so unexpectedly that for a moment it didn't compute. In the back of my mind I was wondering how to let her know what had happened, never for a second thinking that she would already be in the loop.

Intravenous tubes dangled from my hand as I reached for the phone.

'.....Mum?'

'Hel-*loh*!' My mother's familiar voice, thick with distance and emotion. I remember the sound of it. And how surreal it felt, to be here, in the most implausible scenario in which to find myself, yet on the phone with my mum. I was very confused.

'How did you know I was here?'

'We've been looking for you! Everybody's been looking for you!' I couldn't tell if the lilt in her voice was her laughing or crying. I think it might have been both. I understood the feeling.

All this time I thought nobody else had been aware of my disappearance, that nobody had even noticed. Only now did I start to learn how much had been going on in my absence.

I had known, in my heart of hearts, that the only way I was getting out of that canyon alive was if someone noticed I was incommunicado and checked in with Natalie and Lou. I figured above all else, it was those two who needed to notice, because they were, albeit unwittingly, the ones with the vital shard of information about where I had gone, and who would most quickly figure it out. And in the end, that's precisely how it happened.

A few people had noticed I was quiet on Instagram. A shameful marker of my existence, but a marker none the less, without which things might not have ended so well. My mum was already growing concerned and had sent me a probing message. A couple of friends had sent casual texts as well. But my own renowned hard-headed independence made it easy for a lack of response to be brushed off as me taking a social-media break, some time to myself, or simply being too engaged in my travels.

It was Natalie who couldn't let it go. She knew how much of a paparazzi I was, particularly when I was travelling, seeing new places, ensconced in the outdoors. She had a niggling, almost sixth sense that my lack of social-media posts was not a deliberate pause. She and Lou began texting me – casual enquiries about the house and the cats at first, and then questioning if I was OK. Nat then sent Jo and Jef to the house to check on me...Of course, I wasn't there. And neither was the car.

By late Friday morning, I was officially reported missing.

A poster was swiftly put out around the Joshua Tree area and on local Facebook groups with my photo and description. The local search and rescue team had been spurred into action. My parents in New Zealand and my brother Chris in Australia had all been informed. Natalie had reached out to Caroline in Toronto and other friends in the UK and North America. They were looped in on group messages, each of them on the case to figure out where I might have gone.

Telli knew my iCloud log-in and together my friends were trying to hack into my iPad, contacting my phone provider, reaching out to anyone I might have been in contact with recently, trying to ping my phone, doing anything to determine my most likely location. Checking that I hadn't simply gone off grid. That I wasn't planning a trip out of town. That I hadn't got off with a boy. That there might be some other, more innocent explanation and that I wasn't – as my casual text to Lou had so ambiguously suggested – somewhere out in the desert. Because if I had gone into the desert, they knew it meant I would already have been out there for a few days.

Jo and Jef searched the house, finding not only me and the car gone but the cats, hungry and cranky, had clearly not had their litter changed in a while. And after rummaging through my things they had eventually stumbled across my handwritten calendar.

'Look at this,' Jef had said, turning to Jo with the piece of paper.

Tuesday: Lost Palms Oasis.

Confirmation.

Then the police found the car.

At this point, all anybody could do was wait for news.

It would take some time for me to piece together everything that had led to my rescue. Tiny shards of what happened were slowly gathered together over the following weeks and months. But that first day, after my phone had been charged at the hospital, and loved ones had begun to make contact with me, the first seeds of realization were planted. That all this time I had never really been alone.

My first visitor was Alison, who came to Palm Springs early

the next morning. It was so good to see someone I recognized, bringing me back into the world I thought I had lost. To think we'd been sitting having micheladas a week ago and now she was here, sitting against the wall of the ICU as I lay broken on a gurney. She brought me pencils, a sketchpad, a book about John and Yoko. Things to keep me occupied. Distracted from the pain, which is what I needed more than anything.

She was still there when three nurses appeared at the sides of my bed.

'We're here to roll you, we need to clean your back.'

But...I thought that part was over.

'I can't roll, I can't...'

'We'll do it very carefully, and it'll be very quick...'

'No no no no...' I felt panic rising in my chest.

'Honey, you have stones in your back, we need to clean you to avoid you getting a skin infection.'

'I'll risk the infection.'

I was being completely serious. The nurses looked at each other, concerned.

'We have to do it, I'm sorry.'

'Could you knock me out or something?'

'We can't sedate you at the moment.'

'Could I get some more morphine?'

'We can't give you any more than you're already on.'

Jesus. Really? How did it still hurt so much?

'Is there anything at all you can you give me?'

Now their faces were apologetic.

One of them gave me a pillow.

'Oh, honey. You can scream into this.'

———

Three days after I was brought out of the desert, I had surgery on my pelvis. I was wheeled into the operating theatre where the doctor walked me through the procedure. It would be quick, he said. He would be inserting two large titanium pins through my hip, permanent fixtures to secure the pieces of my pelvis back together.

'Hey,' he said, pointing a finger at me, pistol-style. 'What music shall we fix you up to?'

I went under to the sound of Muddy Waters.

As my body was being rebuilt and reinforced, so was my life.

And my new life was, rather wonderfully, full of people.

My friend Tessa flew in from Chicago the day of my surgery; her grinning face was beside me as they wheeled me into my new ward. Jo and Jef arrived, bringing, in lieu of flowers, a whole pineapple. Caroline flew down from Toronto. My mother was already mid-air, on her way from New Zealand. Nat and Lou were waitlist-hopping flights to get back from Scotland. When they finally arrived, Nat came rushing into my room in floods of tears and threw her arms around me. There is no hug tight enough, no thank you big enough, to give the person who saved your life. I felt she was as embedded in me as the pins in my bones.

Beautiful messages came in from perfect strangers. And Tom, from the tattoo shop, drove out to Palm Springs to visit and replaced my ear piercing, which had become red and inflamed.

'Christ, girl, I told you to keep this thing clean,' he joked.

Jean-Paul from the bookshop sent over a copy of Steinbeck's *Travels with Charley*, with a note:

'The desert is brutal, but you are stronger.'

The kindness of people hit me like the weight of a truck, making me cry – really cry – on a daily basis, but it was a joyous weight, one that pinned me to the earth and made me feel secure, anchoring me.

I used to think it was my anxiety and depression that was causing me to turn away from the world, and retreat, but I was beginning to see things differently.

Perhaps it had always been the other way around.

'I can't believe how good you seem,' my mother said, as I joked about with the nurses. Caroline remarked at how I was practically supporting all of *them* more than the other way around. Perhaps it was the sudden appreciation for every single tiny wonderful thing, or perhaps it was the truckload of morphine I was getting but, frankly, I'd never felt better.

Emotionally speaking, at least. Physically, I was a mess. I had sustained multiple traumatic fractures in my pelvis and sacrum (it was while reading my hospital report that I first learned the word 'comminuted': *reduced to splinters*). There were bone fragments in my pelvic joint. Hematomas. I'd severely sprained my left ankle, which was now a Van Gogh swirl of black and blue, and had a fracture that ran from my big toe into the centre of my foot. Blood tests confirmed inflammation in the kidneys and muscle tissue. Severe dehydration. And none of this was surprising – I had felt it. All of it. The pains in my body were as clear as the words written on my medical sheet.

But I couldn't get over how lucky I was to get away with only this much injury. The angle at which I fell and the point at which I landed were nothing but a simple twist of fate. An inch or two could have been the difference between hitting my head and not hitting my head, between my spine meeting and missing rock. Inches away from paralysis. Or death.

I was a mess, but I was a lucky mess. A grateful mess.

I had a second chance now, and this life, this new and brilliant second life, would not be like the one before. Then, I lived in an emotional fortress, a sanctuary in which I could be safe from the things that I was afraid of, but which was also keeping the good and the great out too. It had become an obstacle to connections. This whole time I was locking myself in my room with my fears. It was time to put an end to this.

In this life, I would be open.

After my surgery, I could sit up for the first time. And, for the first time, I could see my legs – uneven stripes of tan and red, patches of sunburn in a couple of places now starting to scab. For the most part, though, they were in surprisingly good shape, my efforts to protect them had paid off.

There were little achievements to tick off, each one a mountain. It would be another few days before I would try using a commode, not that my body was ready for it – I still had no appetite and existed on a diet of jelly and protein shakes, the nurses studiously noting down everything I left on my tray. I graduated from a catheter to a urinal jug, although I required two, such was the volume of fluids being piped through my body around the clock. (Thankfully, by this stage, I'd become something of a master at peeing while lying down.)

I felt delight at the smallest things. The palm trees I could see through the window. The instant coffee a nurse brought me one morning tasted like something divine. I felt like love was oozing through my veins, so thick and fast that I felt the greatest affection for everyone in my orbit. I learned the names of all the nurses who took care of me, jovially introducing them to my friends as if we were all down at the saloon.

Sure, maybe the morphine did have something to do with it. But my new appreciation for simply being alive was intense all on its own. The days in the hospital formed a strange but joyous bubble to exist in, removed from all realities I had previously known. I was lying in limbo, the ward a holding pen between one life and the next.

My travel insurer had confirmed they would take care of all hospital costs, and I was now indescribably grateful that my fear of snakebites had provoked my opting for unlimited medical cover. They were trying to find me a bed in a rehabilitation facility back in Toronto, my current 'place of residence', albeit on paper only. I hadn't had a chance to set up a home there yet, and in truth I wasn't sure where I really belonged.

After a week at my bedside, Mum reluctantly had to go back to New Zealand. I assured her I would soon be off to Canada, for ongoing rehabilitation.

'Be ready,' they said. 'As soon as we get a bed for you, we'll be medevac-ing you'. They were very keen to hand me over to my Canadian insurer, even though the latter would not promise coverage for the billing of my ongoing care.

Friends set up a GoFundMe. This in itself was testing my ability to allow others to offer help and to receive it. But the generosity of people around the world blew me away. I read every message that came through via donations or on social media, each one a little shot of love and kindness. I developed a routine: in the very early hours of the morning, after the nurses woke me to check my vitals, I would lie there until sunrise and, in the brief pocket of being completely alone, write back to every person who had taken time to get in touch to thank them for their donation, my heart feeling like it might burst with the unexpected barrage of kindness. By simply being alive and well I had so much desire to give back what I could, even if a response was all I could offer. I cried a lot in those early hours.

Eighteen days in hospital, and still waiting on the medevac, I received a curt email from my travel insurer announcing that they were retracting the promised coverage. They reasoned that I didn't yet have public healthcare in Canada, even though this had not been a requirement of the application, and was mentioned nowhere in the print. The amount they were now offering up wasn't even enough to cover one day in the bed I was lying in, let alone any of the treatment or medication I was receiving. And they wouldn't budge. I thought I had done everything right, taken out all the things I needed to take out – I thought I was safe now.

Lou came straight to the hospital.

'We're getting you out of here today,' he said.

I was still not eating solids, still not ready to leave, but I had to discharge myself into the care of my friends. I could feel the old me squirming at being a burden on them, but the new me...well, she didn't have many options.

Lou's trusty old Mini was loaded up with my wheelchair,

walker, crutches, shower seat and various medical accoutrements, and he drove us back to their house on the hill in Joshua Tree. It was heading towards sundown as the car pulled into their street. I hadn't been back since the morning I left for the hike, pulling out of this same street, in this same car. The morning I stopped the car to go back for the hiking stick – a move that ultimately saved my life. It felt like a lifetime ago, and yet...as if it had just happened.

JOSHUA TREE

Out of the cocoon of the hospital ward, removed from the steady rush of drugs, I was facing the real world for the first time since the fall. Everything felt different. I had changed, somehow. Inside I felt reborn, while physically I felt trapped – confined to a wheelchair, fully reliant on others. This was the first moment that the reality of what had happened to me, and what I had gone through, actually hit home. I felt a wave of something cold sink over me and by the time Nat bundled me into the guest room – which they'd turned into a temporary care ward – the wave crashed in and I broke down in tears. Lying on the bed, the flashbacks began to crash over me like a relentless wave.

I was back on the boulder. I was sliding. I was reliving the moment I fell – over, and over, and over; I hit the ground again and again and again, feeling that bone-shattering pain and then the gut-wrenching terror of not being able to get up.

Mum had told me this might happen.

'You were so amazing in the hospital but I always figured you were either super-human or the adrenaline of surviving was still coursing through your veins,' she messaged. 'You have been through a major life-changing experience that most people will never experience. It must begin to do things in your mind at some point. I can testify that playing "I'm OK" is not OK!'

How did she know?

She wasn't wrong about the adrenaline. That, along with the bubble of care and constant medication, had been what had helped me get through this so far. I had been safe in the hospital. Every time the pain became too much, I'd press a call button and moments later a shot of morphine would be pressed into the crook of my elbow, the sweet, cold feeling as it hit my veins perhaps the most delicious sensation I had ever experienced.

Now, my friends were forced to play nurse, and I was having to be my own medic, managing pain myself. My nightstand looked like a pick-and-mix candy station of opiates, anticonvulsants, muscle relaxants, sleep-aids, stool-softeners, with my trusty antidepressants tucked amongst them. Natalie helped me inject my own shots of an anticoagulant, pulling my arm taut while I stuck in the needle.

I could still not bear the nerve pain that shot down my left side, setting my foot on fire; I'd soak it in a mixing bowl of ice cubes and water. My iPhone had about seven different alarms set, reminding me to take various pills or shots at different intervals throughout the day and night, ensuring I took the right meds in the right order at the right time. I felt like I was morphing into one of the plastic pill jars, practically rattling when I moved.

The guilt of having friends take care of me was as visceral as it was back when Telli was hanging my sling, only this time, I really couldn't fend for myself. This would be the first of many tests that challenged that deep discomfort I felt when I let people help me. It was training, in a way, to leave the old habits behind.

There was also the guilt I felt for suffering and complaining when I should just be bloody well thankful I wasn't dead. Not gonna lie, that one was a little trickier to overcome.

But every day offered new challenges, as I tested the physical and emotional waters of healing. It was slow going, as was getting about with a wheelchair. The physical therapist had got me practising being upright, using a walking frame for short distances, although the pain and exertion of it was wearing, and it would be three months before my left leg could bear any weight.

'You should try the crutches again,' Lou said, determined it would make it easier to move around, but I was far too afraid of falling. Each time I tried to walk with the crutches one wobble would set me off – the very real horror of slipping and hurting myself all over again making my blood run cold.

'That's pain trauma,' one doctor had explained. 'Your brain remembers and is trying to stop it from happening again.'

You're telling me.

I'd felt safe in the hospital. This felt like muddling through.

CANADA

My family wanted me to come back to New Zealand, but I knew there was no way I could cope with the 20-hour plane journey in the state I was in. So, Mum came to me. She returned to California and escorted me back to Toronto, a DIY medevac of sorts, setting my friends free of the burden of being my carers.

We rented a small, overpriced apartment in downtown Toronto, near the hospital – the only place I could find last minute, in the height of summer, that could accommodate my wheelchair and specific needs, such as a shower big enough for me to get in and out of myself, lowering myself from my chair to the shower seat.

For weeks my mum wheeled me back and forth to hospital and doctor's appointments, for X-rays, physio and scans. She fed me, although thanks to the glut of opiates and other pills I still had no appetite. She pushed me outside to feed the squirrels, even though I was too exhausted and too sore to be interested in doing anything. She called my dad and my uncle and all the folks back home to keep them updated on my progress. I'd never leaned so heavily on my mother before...

I'd never leaned so heavily on *anyone*.

Unfortunately I was also leaning very heavily on opioids. Without realizing the impact, I was struggling with an increased attachment to Percocet, blithely unaware of the severity of its addictiveness. The discharge nurse had mentioned this was a risk but seemed to think I was responsible enough to not abuse them. And she was right. But responsibility has nothing to do with it. This was a drug, which my body learned to depend on to simply not suffer. I'd never heard of Percocet before all of this; I knew nothing of the widespread opioid crisis. I certainly had no idea just how terrifyingly easy it is to form a reliance on them. All I knew that the white pills in the orange jar were the only thing that softened the pain in my body, that allowed me to function in a way that resembled normal, and I relied on them heavily to be able to leave the house. To make it through a day.

Nat had warned me, too – 'You'll get addicted,' she'd said. But I'd laughed it off, like the idea was silly. It seemed too far-fetched to think I would *actually* get addicted to prescription medication.

It's hard to put yourself in the picture sometimes.

I was going to the walk-in clinic, seeing new doctors every time. It must have been doctor number six, maybe seven, who finally shut it down.

'You're taking a very high dosage of Percocet. *And* Gabapentin.'

He looked up from his notes, his face full of concern, and I nodded, affirming for the hundredth time the list of things I'd been prescribed. *Yep. All of those things.*

'You do realize that taking these together, and at these levels, can be fatal.'

My mother's face reflected the horror in mine. I'd been taking that combination for two months. Once out of hospital there had been no guidance, just more pieces of paper that I could exchange for more pills.

'You need to come off Percocet as soon as you can.'

He gave me a week.

I panicked, halved my hefty dose immediately – and crashed like a tonne of bricks. I was trying to quickly wean myself off something I hadn't even realized I was addicted to. My bones aching, my nerves on fire, I was unable to keep what little food I ate in my stomach, suffered anxiety attacks and regularly broke down in tears. We went back to the clinic. Another different doctor. This time, he gave me an off-ramp of one month.

'Healing isn't linear,' Mum remarked one day. That stuck with me. I wrote it down and reminded myself of this every time I felt despondent.

While I was busy trying to get myself better, global media continued to prod me almost daily, keen for updates and interviews, ranging from polite requests in my DMs to constant cold-calling of my relatives. Friends and family members sent me photos of newspaper articles about my accident.

'Trust a Nelson to be famous for falling over,' Chris had messaged, which made me laugh.

The attention felt surreal. They wanted details. Especially about drinking urine – it was what the headlines led with. I didn't have the mental or physical energy to face any of it, but I agreed to a couple of interviews to the most respectful requests. The majority I declined. I was exhausted, I just wanted to lie down and go to sleep for a few months and wake up healed.

There was one request, however, that I didn't feel I could ignore: an email from a journalist covering the disappearance of another hiker in Joshua Tree National Park. He had already been missing for three weeks. I knew the trail he had been on – it was one I had hiked myself. The journalist wanted my perspective: could I tell them what it's like out there in the park? As someone

who has survived? And, perhaps, I might offer some words of
hope for the family?

My first instinct was to say, 'Of course, whatever I can do to
help.' I felt so bereft for this man and for his loved ones. Surely,
this was my responsibility, to give back, any way I possibly could.
But there were sinking pangs of guilt – guilt that I had made it
out, while he was still out there. And then the realization that
there was nothing I could say to his loved ones that would help
them. Who was I to make such bold statements? He had been out
there so long already, the temperatures even hotter than when I
was out there; I could not offer them solace. I didn't know how
much hope I could give to anyone. I wrote back to the journalist,
declining to comment.

But now I couldn't stop thinking about the missing man. I sat
slumped in my wheelchair looking out the apartment window.
The sun started to set over the high-rise buildings of downtown,
the distant wail of city sirens ever present, and my mind returned
to the desert. How it had looked at this time of the day. The time
before dusk, when the shadows moved over the boulders and the
sky began to fade from blue to grey, and then to black. How it
had felt every time I faced going into a long, dark night ahead.
I thought of him still out there. I felt a chill as my blood turned
cold. I started to shiver and broke down in tears, sobbing heavily
into the few spoonfuls of pasta my mother had urged me to eat.

'Tears are emotions escaping,' I heard her say. 'What's the
emotion you're feeling?'

My mum's question surprised me: I wasn't used to us talking
about feelings in this way. Not with my parents. I had kept my
anxiety and emotional messiness hidden away all these years, not

used to bringing them into the light. But something had shifted. This life was different. Stoicism had moved aside.

'Fear,' I gulped between sobs. 'It's fear.'

If tears were emotions escaping, then that explains why I found it so hard to cry. I'd had my feelings on maximum security lockdown for a long time.

But now I couldn't hold them in. Not any more. I was as vulnerable as I had ever been, and what's more, this side of me was being seen. And I found that being seen in a state of weakness did not take away from my strength. I had survived four days in the desert. I was strong. I didn't have to prove that by hiding my vulnerability. I had to make space for the changes I needed to make, no matter how uncomfortable it might be.

Two days after my last dose of Percocet, I celebrated my thirty-sixth birthday.

'I'm ready,' I told my family. 'I'm ready to go back to New Zealand.'

It was time to heal on solid ground.

NEW ZEALAND

How strange it was, being back in New Zealand. I'd only just left the UK, heading for Canada. And ended up in California. And now, I was here. Talk about veering from the trail...I was as far off my route as I could get.

I have to admit, there was a part of me reluctant to come back. It was a discomfort always felt on home soil. A discomfort, I suppose, in having to face my old self. To be reminded of that 'weaker' Claire. Because, in a way, this is where I had kept her, all this time. Let her remain invisible and left her for dust in the arse-end of the world while I carried on without her.

Well, I knew how that worked out.

As it turns out, I needed that Claire. And maybe this was the opportunity I needed to finally learn to accept her. To not just acknowledge her, but *see* her.

And she needed strong Claire to come back to her.

There was a family reunion lunch. I got to hug my dad, who had arrived wielding a belated birthday cake for me. 'Did someone say there was a party?' We all ate slices of chocolate gateau on our laps in my cousin's living room, through the window, a view of the wild and windy sea. The same one I'd grown up beside.

I had never felt more grateful to be there. I appreciated, at last, that this little island might be far away from the world I knew, but it wasn't a place I had to escape from. It was a place I could escape to. How lucky I was to have that.

And it was the perfect place to recover. I didn't have anywhere to go. And not only because of my mobility limitation, but because...there really was nowhere to go. Nothing around my parents' house but more houses and fields, dotted with cows and wandering pukekos. Anxiety set in as I wondered how I would keep myself entertained while unable to go anywhere or do anything. Months of being on the other side of the world from the life I knew, from my friends and familiar faces and places. Months in the drizzling New Zealand winter, in the middle of the countryside, with just the birdsong and the clockwork rhythm of my parents' daily routines.

I had learned how to use crutches, which was useful at times, but I was still weeks away from putting weight on my left side. I rolled about the house in a compact blue wheelchair that Tony, my stepdad, had rented for me; one which would fit through the doors and hallway and which, I noticed with some bemusement, had the ominous brand name 'Karma'.

'You need to learn how to be bored,' said Mum, as I sat in my Karma, strong-arming my parent's old ginger cat on to my lap and wondering what to do with myself. I realized she was right.

I'd become that child again, growing up by the sea, whining, 'Mum, we're bored!'

And it was always the same: 'You kids have got the whole beach out there, how can you be bored? Go find something to do.'

The thing is, eventually we *would* find something to busy ourselves with – imaginations forced to kick in and figure it out. Boredom! I'd forgotten how to do it. It was time to retrain in being bored. To let my imagination stretch its legs again, the antidote to the habits I'd got into of losing hours to mindless scrolling, my poor attention span shrunken like an old, discarded piece of fruit.

It was time to stop searching for distraction. I needed to learn how to just be.

So, in the months that followed, I made time for boredom. And it wasn't as boring as I'd expected. Sometimes I did absolutely nothing but gaze out of the window, watching signs of nature twitch about in the garden. I found such affection for watching the bees bumbling around Mum's flower garden. When I spied on the fantails and sparrows that squabbled in the cabbage tree it was as if I was watching a TV drama. Every little detail seemed sharper now, like I was looking at the world through brand new lenses, very aware that the world could have gone on turning without me, only I was here and watching it turn.

I also read more books. I wrote more frequently. I rummaged through my late nana's knitting bag and taught myself how to crochet.

Every weekend, Dad picked me up for a long drive around the countryside; we'd listen to blues music, like we used to do when I was young, and look for different cafés to go to. 'Gotta Instagram those coffees,' we'd joke. For the first time in a long time I was taking life slowly and enjoying the moment, the people, the sense of being here – not just here, in New Zealand, but *here*. Living. There was nowhere I needed to be but exactly where I was. How much easier it was to appreciate things when it had almost all been taken away from me.

My only other regular appointment was with Ash, the local physiotherapist, who would help get me back on my feet, something I was impatiently eager for. I had lost a lot of weight from the opioids, which had killed my appetite, and every morning as I got dressed I'd lean on my crutches in front of the mirror and try to connect the visible changes with what had happened. Months on, there was still the bright pink slash of sunburn across my belly, and the purple scar from my surgery, but what struck me was how thin I'd got. I was skinnier than I'd ever seen myself.

'Your backside has probably disappeared,' said Ash. And he was right, my bum was as flat as a pancake, my glutes entirely withered away. Before all of this happened I might have relished this much slimmer version of me, but now all I wanted was my strength back. I wanted to hike again. That desire certainly hadn't changed, other than being ignited with new fervour.

I had a goal. I wanted to finish the trail that almost finished me.

From the moment I learned I was going to survive, I knew I would go back for the Lost Palms Oasis. That I would return to the trail, and this time make it to the end. I was determined to stand at the foot of those palms.

It had become, over the months of recovery, the goal post, standing in the distance, coaxing me to studiously focus on the steady rebuilding of my strength, to heal. To be patient. Which, of course, is something I've never been very good at. But I learned. Impatience now would only set me back. I wanted this too much – if I was going to heal, I had to do it right.

And things were certainly progressing. After three months, my pelvis could bear my weight again and Ash had me standing on both legs for the first time. The moment I stood unaided, letting my weight fall on both feet, had felt strange, as if I was floating rather than simply standing up. My recovery grew more determined from there. Over the next few weeks, I graduated from my wheelchair to full-time crutches. I thought I had appreciated my body before, but now I looked at it in a completely new light.

I had twice-weekly physio. Lots of rest. Within a month of taking that first stand, Ash had me walk across the gym floor with one crutch. Then with no crutches. As soon as I could stand unaided, he had me doing squats on a wobble board. There was leg work, cycling, stretches, I groaned and gritted my teeth through it all; it was gruelling.

'One more,' he'd promise.

Then he'd always add, 'And…one more for good luck,' to which I would screw my face up and groan. But I could feel my muscles coming back to life, my body growing in strength with every move I made. And as I became stronger, so did my ever-increasing determination to regain my independence.

I took it as a personal victory that my wheelchair was returned to the rental office almost three weeks earlier than planned.

'Are you sure?' Tony had asked, keen to be rid of it too, but only if I was.

'Yes, I'm done.'

I had made my peace with Karma.

But had I made my peace with the desert?

Did I ever want to go back?

And would I ever want to go hiking again?

These were questions I was asked a lot, by friends, family members or strangers on the internet. The answer was always a definitive *yes*. I love hiking. I love the desert. Why, having been given a second chance at life, would I do the things I love less, when I could do them more? Why would I want to spend it hiding or living behind fear? That was precisely how I had been living my life before all of this.

When you realize how much time you've wasted on fear, you sure as hell don't want to spend any more of it being afraid.

JOSHUA TREE

The day I drove back in to Joshua Tree felt like coming home. It had been six hard months since I'd left this place, and I hadn't realized how much I'd missed it. Driving in from Palm Springs airport, through the sea of rolling wind turbines, the familiar watercoloured mountains in the rear-view mirror and that same old favourite driving playlist on the rental car stereo, I found myself spilling over with emotion. Properly crying, like a lunatic.

They were happy tears.

I'd come back to finish a few things. Or start them, depending which way you looked at it. I now felt a visceral connection with the place and the people in it, like it was part of the scar tissue on my body. I wanted to finish the hike to the oasis. To be reunited with Natalie and Lou, to hug them – properly, standing up – for the first time since the fall. To see Jo, Jef, Alison and Bryan, all the friends I had made there and had sorely missed.

It felt so easy slipping back: the very next morning we were drinking breakfast Bloody Marys down at the saloon, shooting shit with the locals, like nothing had changed. Except so much had changed, for me. I felt like my life was now split into Before and After. And everything After felt like a bonus. In every tiny, trivial detail there was something to appreciate. I loved the After. Also, the After had a lot more people in it.

Like Manny and Eric. My rescuers. I'd only met them once, but they meant the world to me. And now it was time to reconnect.

A week after arriving, I arranged to meet Manny and his wife Theresa for dinner. I had barely limped into the restaurant when this tall, grinning man appeared, embracing me in a bear hug so enthusiastic he lifted me right off the ground.

'Hey, you clean up all right, you know!' he laughed as we walked to the table.

'Yeah, well, you guys didn't catch me at my best.'

His voice was still burned into my brain, those incredible words from the helicopter impossible to forget. It was weird, I felt an affinity with this person, as if I'd known him for a long time. Manny and Theresa were like family; we talked for so long we almost forgot to order food. I had so many questions for Manny – about his job, about what it takes to go searching for missing people, and what it's like when, more often than not, you're retrieving people whose story ended so differently from mine.

He told me the story of the call out and the rescue, but in more detail this time. I still struggled to grasp just what they had been up against. Manny shuffled in his seat, for a moment seeming embarrassed. And then he told me that he had photos. Of the rescue. 'Everything about that situation was so crazy, I had to capture it,' he explained. He hoped I wasn't upset that he'd done so...

But did I want to see them?

There were photos?

Photos from the best day of my life?

Of course I wanted to see them!

As I looked at the images of the rescue I understood now about the logistics of landing their helicopter in the difficult the terrain. Where they'd hiked down to reach me. How the California Highway Patrol helicopter had manoeuvred their chopper into the canyon in the high winds. And, once I had been safely extricated, Manny had captured a bird's-eye view of where they had found me. If I hadn't seen the photo I'd scarcely have believed it myself. I was there, I knew I had got lost, but to see just how remote I had been sent a chill up my spine. The photo showed nothing but vast, seemingly endless rocky desert, with Manny's finger indicating something. As I looked closer I made out a small black dot within the sea of rock – the hole I had fallen into. The hole in which he'd seen the tiniest flicker of movement, my hat atop the plastic bag at the end of a stick.

How? How had he seen me?

There was only one photo of me, taken for posterity. Dark, in the shadow of the rock, taken when my head was turned away and eyes closed against the dust from the helicopter blowing about. I was gaunt, my hands clutching a water bottle to my belly. That image threw me.

That's what I would've looked like if I'd died, I thought.

That's how I would've looked if my body had been found.

I had accepted death was coming to me, and this photo made me understand I was still processing that. It was like looking at myself post mortem, as if I had stumbled through the canyon and come across my own body. Seeing it made the reality of my sitting here, alive and well, feel all the more surreal.

'I'm glad you took these. I really am,' I said. 'And if it makes you feel any better, I would've done the exact same thing.' Which was true.

Theresa nodded towards Manny. 'He's always taking photos,' she said.

'Yeah, always capturing the moment!' Manny laughed.

I couldn't help smiling.

So he's a paparazzo too.

A week later, I drove out to visit the whole aviation unit, where I was reunited with Eric and got to meet the rest of the crew. Over slices of pizza they told me their side of the story of the day they'd gone out searching for me, filling in the gaps of the rescue.

'When we found you we thought, "That girl won't walk again",' said Eric, in a rare moment of sombreness. Then he leaned back in his chair and waved his arms in my direction.

'But man, I'm sure as hell glad we were wrong!'

Eating pizza in a hangar with this welcoming bunch of cops was a situation I could never, ever have foreseen. Yet it felt so normal. It was crazy, but good crazy. Life was suddenly sewn together by all these threads, connections, the ease and joy of it feeling overwhelming at times. I found comfort being around the two people who had spent time in that canyon with me. It connected us.

'Friends for life!' we'd all exclaimed, exchanging goodbye hugs. And we meant it. We really meant it.

When I drove back to the desert, following the highway as it cut through the painted hills and the sea of wind turbines, I was taken aback by the tears that had poured out of me. This seemed to be a new thing for me, this crying in cars, I thought. In fact, crying this much at all. *Tears are emotions escaping.* It was only later that I realized what I was releasing was the excess loneliness that I no longer needed. It no longer served me. This life I was now living was so open and ready for greater connections, and I could appreciate each and every one with a level of gratitude I'd never known was possible.

It was now January, the new year; a recent slough of rain had soaked the desert, the air spritzed and fresh, heavy with the earthy scent of creosote and sage. Like the emptiness and the sound of the coyotes, this smell was one of my favourite details of the desert.

When it rains in Joshua Tree, it really goes for it. Roads in town flood, potholes gush over, and the rising water levels threaten to close Old Woman Springs Road, its undulating dips slowly drowning. Wild and bitter biting winds had set across the region for weeks, making hiking unappetizing and requiring a full regalia of winter clothing just to get to the shops. On top of this, the recent government shut-down had been closing national parks across America, and the chances of Joshua Tree National Park being one of them were looking higher as the days wore on.

But I had marked this particular day in my calendar weeks ago. It had to come together. It simply had to.

That morning we woke to blue skies. Sunshine and mild temperatures. And the park was still open. The conditions were as close to ideal as I could have hoped for, which I took as a wholly positive sign that today we were meant to be doing this. The universe, I supposed, was all for this little expedition. Today we were going to the Lost Palms Oasis.

There were four of us heading out: Jo and Jef, and Caroline, who had flown in from Toronto. It had been difficult to get everyone together at once; Alison, Bryan, Natalie and Lou had all hoped to come but wound up being tied up in work and family commitments. I knew that while having us all there would've been perfect, this was how life is. I had learned to let go of perfect. You don't need to have it all when what you do have is bloody plenty.

And four *was* plenty. When the time came, I was glad not to have too large a group. I was excited, but also a little trepidatious; I had no idea how this hike was going to make me feel. Once, all I wanted was to get out of that place and now I was going back in. Not that I planned to repeat my steps exactly. This hike was not about finding the place I fell. I wasn't ready for that. This was about finishing the trail and reaching the oasis at last.

This was unfinished business.

We picked up sandwiches from the Crossroads Cafe and caffeine from Joshua Tree Coffee and piled into my little rental car. We were stocked with plenty of water and bags of snacks. Jo and Caroline compared trail mix.

'Ooh, cashews, the "limousine of nuts".'

'Why limousine? Because they're long and expensive?'

'I think they were once considered classy, but now they're a bit...common.'

'So definitely a limousine.'

'OK, so what's a peanut then?'

'A Honda Civic.'

Murmurs of agreement.

I smiled. This is what I had fought to live for those days and nights in the desert – talking nonsense with friends. When you come so close to losing everything, it is the smallest things you realise you'd miss the most. And here we were, friends forming connections over trail mix. Talking absolute nonsense about nuts. God, I could have cried again.

The temperature was mild and rising as I drove us across the national park towards the low desert. It was all coming back to me: the turns I had taken that morning, the views over the valley, the tufty fields of the cholla cactus gardens with tiny glints of the morning sun on the pinpoints of their spines. The Cottonwood visitor's centre was not yet open but from there I knew the way to the trail. We parked at the trailhead, not far from where I had parked Lou's Mini last time. Boots were yanked on, laces tied, water bottles filled from the back-up bottles stashed in the trunk and sunscreen generously reapplied. Jef unzipped his hoodie, revealing a new handwritten t-shirt slogan: WHERE'S CLAIRE?

I hooted with laughter.

'I hope you don't find it in bad taste,' he said.

'No way, I'm honoured.' I thought it was bloody brilliant.

This was it, you know. All of it. Friendship. All the wonderful dumb-assery and in-jokes and fun. The remarkable affection of being with people you feel comfortable enough to take the piss out of. For me, that's the gold stuff of life. Connection.

We made our way towards the start of the trail.

'What about Brazil nuts. What car would a Brazil nut be?'

'Something big and sturdy.'

'An Escalade,' said Caroline.

Everyone agreed.

'Definitely an Escalade.'

I was wearing the same boots. Not for any sense of occasion but because they were simply the boots I had, and I loved them. Given all we'd been through, they were as much a part of me as the thick, pink bumps of scar tissue on my heels from where they'd been pressed into them all that time. I also brought the hiking stick. My hip was still healing, the muscles tight and nerve spasms were easily triggered if pressed. But even though the stick was a necessary aid, there was no way I would have come back here without it. Lou had gifted it to me and in return I'd bought him a new one from the same wood carver. Mine he now referred to as the Elder Wand – and who was I to say it didn't have magic in it?

Here I was. Same boots, same stick, same rhythm of walking in the sand. It was the strangest sensation to be back here; the heavy awareness that I might not have been here at all, that I was walking this trail in some parallel existence, seeing both versions of the sliding-door effect. I couldn't help but think of me lying somewhere south of here, isolated and struggling to hang on. I thought of those bleakest moments when I believed I would never again do something like this, never again be back in the land of the living. Then, flat on my back and losing all hope, I could only have dreamed of being up on my feet. But hiking in the desert with friends again...that was more than I could ever have wished for. It was the most discomforting and wonderful and humbling feeling.

Having my friends with me was invaluable, and no doubt what kept the trauma at bay. The views of the landscape were the same as last time, the memories coming back to me as if I'd only been here yesterday, but the fact I was not alone made it different enough. And they checked in with me from time to time.

'You doing OK?' asked Caroline softly, as we trod over a high ridge.

'Yeah, I'm OK.'

I'm fine.

This time, I really was.

The trail flattened out, carefully placed rows of rocks subtly marking the route among the expanse of scrubby earth. But with so many rocks in the terrain, they were not always obvious.

And then we were in the wash. I recognized it – I remembered the high banks on each side and the spiked growth of cacti and brush jutting out and creating shadows over the coarse pale sand. We carried on along it, following the snaking riverbed. It was just as it had been all those months before.

Only this time, I saw the sign.

A small, weathered wooden signpost, no longer than my forearm, was planted jauntily into the ribs of the wash, and on it were the words 'Lost Palms Oasis' and a simple arrow pointing left, indicating to take a turn up the bank.

The turn I hadn't taken.

The sign must have always been there, which means I must simply have been looking in the other direction at the moment of passing it. That's all it would have taken. The sun in my eyes, and a glance the other way at the wrong moment.

Could it have all been that simple?

I felt a lot of things in that moment, but ultimately very foolish and incredibly sad.

Another part of me – somewhere deeper, darker and still healing – felt the pull to pass it by once more, to carry on the way I'd gone the first time, seeking out the path I had taken instead and revisiting the place where I had fallen. That place. Where the desert had swallowed me, where I had been forced to stare my own existence in the eye, to accept my agonizing end.

I shouldn't want to go back there. Yet a part of me did. But I reminded myself that wasn't why we had come. It was too risky, too much at stake. I wasn't ready to put anyone else in that place with me.

I wasn't ready.

Not today.

That said, it did seem wrong to casually pass these crossroads now I had found them again. If I didn't feed my curiosity at least a small tidbit, would I regret it? It might be some time before I was back here.

'Do you guys mind if we go just a little way down the wash? Just to see?'

The others agreed; I am sure everyone was just as curious as I was. And sure enough, only a moment later we came to a passage in the rock where the wash narrowed and the ground level dropped substantially.

God. I remembered it now. The moment I jumped down. The crack of the water bottle as it broke on the sand. This was it, this was where I should have turned back, when it all might have gone so differently – a hike completed like all the other hikes before it, enjoyed but inconsequential, overall, filed away in my travel memories, a few snapshots shared on an Instagram feed.

I stood and stared at the opening in the rock, and at the lower wash that fell beyond it. The gap seemed so much narrower this time; the drop so much further down. But the last time I came to this place I had felt so at ease. Strange to think of that now. I'd not felt any inkling that I was anywhere but on the trail. And I had simply hopped down. Carried on. Headed towards an experience I could never have presumed or imagined.

The four of us stopped at the passage, shrugged off our daypacks, seated ourselves against the tall, pale rocks, and took a moment to gather thoughts. The mood was weirdly sombre.

'Vodka?' Jef enquired, whipping out a silver hip flask.

'YES. And I've got whisky,' I said, pulling out another. The flasks were passed around, nips taken, everyone subdued in quiet contemplation. The whisky was a balm to the burning discomfort I felt, the heaviness in my chest loosened a bit by the dram. Jo placed a hand on my arm for a moment. And for a minute or two, nobody spoke. Nothing needed to be said. It was me who, in the end, felt the need to break the silence.

'Sorry guys, I know this is a bit strange,' I said.

'Uh, of course this is fucking strange,' said Jef. 'But that's why we're here.'

I could not have been more grateful for my companions. Each of these three people naturally possess bucketloads of empathy and understanding, things that I really needed right now. With the trust and gratitude I felt for them, I could not have felt in safer hands. Each of them knew how to help me tread this path – whether they realized it or not.

The flasks did one more round as we all took a final nip for the road.

'OK,' I said, pulling myself to my feet. 'Let's get back on the trail.'

With every step I felt a heady sense of being fully present, observing myself putting one foot in front of the other. Those four days lying out here, looking up, and wondering – what if? Now, it was as if I was floating above myself, looking down at the four of us walking this trail, and finally answering that question for myself.

What if?

What if I survived?

I would be here. Doing precisely this. Making my way back.

After almost four hot, hilly miles, there it was. What we had come for. The Lost Palms Oasis. Stepping up the rise, I saw it, across the valley ahead. From out of this harsh, dry landscape, a group of lush palm trees rose up, tucked together amongst the vast, rocky desert. It was incredible. And maybe it seemed especially so under these particular circumstances, but to me it was like stumbling across Sir Arthur Conan Doyle's lost world.

My first attempt to reach this oasis had almost killed me. And now I was standing before it. The others gathered behind me. And for a moment we simply stopped. And stared. We had really made it.

A little exploring found a path down the cliff. With a bit of careful scrambling down a trail scattered with scree and loose rock, manoeuvring ourselves around jutting boulders, one by one we arrived. On solid ground. Standing at the foot of the palms.

Above us, the towering trees loomed high, palm branches stretched wide like wings, sheltering us from the sun's glare with a gentle shade. The trunks were encased in thick layers of leaves it had long since shed, some covered all the way to the ground, making them look like shaggy, benevolent monsters. I gazed up at them, awestruck.

It had been real. All of it. The falling, the crack, the breaking of bones and those four days and three nights trapped out here in the loneliest place on earth. The rescue, the recovery and the realizations that followed. Standing here, it would be easy to think it had all been some peculiar dream.

But I had never been more awake.

THINGS I LEARNED FROM FALLING

I wish I could say I walked out of that desert a new and improved version of myself.

If only it were as simple as being offered a clean slate and starting over entirely.

That's not how living works. If I've learned anything it's that our faults and failures are as much a part of who we are as the great and agreeable bits. Coming close to death and out the other side hasn't made those less palatable parts of me disappear, but it has forced me to see the whole person I am. And to accept her.

For so long I had been denying my needs because they didn't fit the version of me I *wanted* to be; what I needed and what I wanted to need did not always match. You know that saying, that comparison is the thief of joy? To me, it's expectation. I'd expected so much of my life – and of myself – to be a certain way, and I lived on the knife-edge of fear about being disappointed: a battle that, had I continued to try and fight, would leave me hollow. I've set no such expectations now. After this, what is given to me is more than I probably deserve. Finally, expectation can make way for acceptance, and that Hokusai's wave of gratitude that is now crashing in.

I now understand that the loneliness and isolation I was feeling was never about my relationships, my social circumstance or, indeed, anything external. My loneliness is something inside of me, something built in. Whatever far-flung corner of the world I moved on to, it would have shown up there too. It was going to follow me wherever I went, because I was feeding it.

By swallowing my pain and fear of failure, and keeping people out, I was only shutting myself in, and shutting myself off from connection and everything that is possible. All this time I longed to be seen, but how was anyone going to see me if I was in hiding? Shutting myself in that room, behind walls. Showing only the parts of me I thought were worth seeing.

All this time I had felt fear in all the wrong places. Anxiety and panic and doubt had become constant bedfellows, setting up camp in my head and holding me back in my relationships and creative expression...yet I went hiking over boulders in the desert completely alone and I was not afraid; I sensed no risk. The only thing I should really have been afraid of was the one thing that didn't scare me.

God, fear is such a waste of time, isn't it?

I know we can't exactly live without it, and it will still turn up where it serves no good purpose, but I can recognize it, acknowledge it, remind myself I have felt real fear before, and this isn't it. I think of the canyon and tell myself: *Right here, right now, I am OK.*

There is so much strength in vulnerability. I realize, now, that being vulnerable is not going to kill me. But trying not to be vulnerable almost did.

Incredibly, each of us is installed with technology that has one function: to keep us alive. Every day our body will fight to survive. And if broken it will heal. It also has an incredibly reliable notification system, so when something is out of balance, it lets you know. The tension of emotion, the weariness of stress, the craving for wide open spaces...When it's telling me something I now know I really need to listen.

I'm still flawed. I still feel irritated by terribly trivial things. I still constantly wrestle with my emotions. I have hard days and moments of weakness. I still feel safest in my own little space. I see myself falling into old patterns, slipping back into the comfort of the familiar – guilt and shame can feel like an easy place to hide.

But now, when I feel like I'm slipping, I have something to kick my boots against. Gratitude. A mountain of it, so large and looming that at any moment I can stretch out a hand and touch the side of the rock. It's always there. Grounding me.

The life we live is an unmarked trail, one of ascents and descents, of changing perspectives and fresh views to take our breath away, along with the constant risks of canyons and slips and phases of inclement weather. By the very nature of the course, mistakes will be made. We will get lost. We will fall. And it will hurt like hell. Sometimes we might question whether we can even carry on. But we walk the trail anyway, because that's what it is not only to exist, but to live. Maybe it's not that we find ourselves by heading for new places, but rather, the journey there gives us the chance to see ourselves more clearly. Around every corner are adventures to be had and new relationships to be started. Sights to be seen. The longer we walk, the easier it is to take them for granted. This trail we have trod since the day we were born becomes so familiar that we often fall into autopilot, forget to stop to look around us, or to look back and consider how far we've already made it.

Complacency kills.

But perhaps it's OK to fall. Through falling we find out not only how strong we are, but how glorious it is to be on the trail at all.

EPILOGUE

Up ahead, the slender palms of Cottonwood Oasis waved gently, announcing that we were almost back at the trailhead. Caroline, Jo, Jef and I, excited at nearing the end of the hike, made plans to go somewhere for a well-earned cold drink. We settled on The Palms, the bar I had meant to go to all those months ago with Alison, since I'd never made it.

Beyond the palm trees it was possible to get a glimpse of the wide sweep of the car park. It hit me then, that this was the way out. Like, the *actual* way out. My mind flashed to the last time I'd left this place – the stretcher, sand whipping through the air, the beating of the helicopter. The indescribable pain. Now it was my boots – and the boots of my friends – that were carrying us out, legs striding, water bottles swinging. I couldn't match the two sequences; every step of this walk felt like treading simultaneously in this life and in another.

As we came back into range, my phone vibrated in my pocket. Texts from my parents, from Manny, Bryan and others, wishing me well. A surge of gratitude threatened to lift me right off the ground.

Suddenly a sound came from somewhere a little way off behind us – so familiar, yet strangely out of place. A shriek; a cry. It was the unmistakable howl of a coyote. The four of us stopped and turned to face the way we had just come, scanning the rolling desert, trying to place the coyote's whereabouts. The yipping grew, the familiar singsong choir rising and elevating, several voices joining together as one. *Dog song.* It was the first time I had ever heard coyotes howling in the daytime.

'They're singing for you,' said Jo softly, peering into the distance.

'It's like they're saying goodbye,' said Caroline.

A tingle ran up my spine. I took a few steps to the side where there was a rise in the dirt, held my hand over my eyes and scanned the horizon, searching for a glimpse of them among the landscape of scrub and juniper, and seeing nothing. They can't have been far – but that was the magic of coyotes, an ability to appear and disappear, to be seen and heard only as they wished.

I didn't admit it to anyone else, but right then and there I got the feeling that, whomever and whatever had been looking out for me, the coyotes knew something about it.

Thank you, I mouthed silently in their direction.

Thank you.

SAFETY TIPS FOR HIKERS

It's a common misconception that hiking is just *walking*. But in wilderness surroundings there are more factors to contend with in addition to putting one foot in front of the other. I did some things right, but others...not so much. It would mean everything if others can learn from my mistakes. Trust me on this much: you're only over-prepared until something goes wrong.

BEFORE YOU GO:

Share your plans

I know, it's hard when you're an independent soul and you don't sense any risk in your route, but this is a big one.

- Tell someone where you're going, when you plan to return, and what time you'll contact them when you're back. Do this even if you're hiking with someone else. It only takes a minute to do but if something goes wrong, it will be the most important text you ever send.
- Go one further and send a photo of yourself before setting off, so if you're lost, search teams know what you're wearing.
- As a back-up, leave a note in the windshield of the car that gives your name, location, date, and instructions to call for help if the car is still there by a certain time.

Don't rely on your phone

- Bring your phone, but prepare as if you won't have it. Whether your device runs out of battery, gets damaged or you find yourself without signal, phoning for help should not be relied upon as your sole means of getting out of trouble.

- If your own mobile network is out of range you can still call emergency services as long as your phone can pick up a signal on another service. But you cannot call *anyone* if you are out of mobile range entirely.
- If you can, consider a GPS-based personal locator beacon as a back-up.

Do your research
- Before you go, speak to park-centre staff, rangers, or hikers who have extensive knowledge of the terrain about how strenuous it is and what to expect, so you can make a measured assessment of your ability.
- Know your limits. You won't enjoy biting off more than you can chew and the chance of incident becomes so much higher if you do.
- Find out what the risks are: are there snakes? Bears? Flash floods? Whatever it is, know how to react and respond to the dangers before you go.
- Get comfortable being in the outdoors. If you plan on hiking regularly, check out local courses in backcountry hiking to get you truly prepared.

ON THE HIKE:
- Every hour or mile, turn around and take in the view, look for landmarks – even take a picture. It's easy to get turned around or lose the trail.

- Don't leave the path. Nobody *means* to get lost, but many casualties come about when someone has strayed from the trail or climbed beyond barriers or markers. Try to minimise the risk.
- Scrambling or climbing up rocks is always much easier than coming down. Descending is more difficult because you can't so easily see where your footing will be placed – and gravity doesn't leave a lot of room for error.
- Turn your phone on airplane mode. You can still use the camera but doing this will preserve the battery in case you do need to call for help (if in service range), to look at your GPS or even to use the torch if you become lost at night.

PACKING TIPS:
- Take more water than you think you'll need: as a guide, calculate for half a litre per hour...and then, chuck in an extra litre. Remember, what you carry is only going to get lighter as you go.
- Don't be tempted to scrimp on sun protection. Slip, slop, slap.
- A whistle can carry further than your voice when trying to attract attention, and you won't shout yourself hoarse.
- Carry a mirror – use it to reflect sunlight so you can signal aircraft, or other people from a distance.
- Pack a warm layer, regardless of the climate. And wear – or at least pack – a brightly coloured item of clothing so you can be more easily spotted if lost.

A FINAL WORD...
National Parks are areas of protected wilderness – this does not mean we are protected in them. The risks remain the same as anywhere in the outdoors.

So stay humble. You can be prepared for anything, but you cannot be prepared for everything.

With thanks to Joshua Tree Search & Rescue (in conjunction with friendsofjosh.org), Eric Hannum at Riverside County Sheriff and Richard Adams of the California Highway Patrol for their contributions to this list.

ACKNOWLEDGEMENTS

That my book ends on a note of thanks was not accidental; it is a thank you that belongs to so many.

Firstly, there would not be a book at all had I never been rescued. Natalie Saunders and Lou Litrenta, I am beyond thankful for your instinct and action that day, and for your generosity of care in those weeks that followed. For that, you will have my gratitude always. I do hope the cats have forgiven me.

I'm eternally thankful to Manny Romero and Eric Bashta of the Riverside County Sheriff Aviation unit, who found me in the absolute middle of nowhere. What a joy to write about that day. (And see? I told you I'd keep the 'fuckin' coyote' part in!) Friends for life.

My thanks and admiration also go out to Jen Earle, Chad Thomas and Richard Adams of the California Highway Patrol, who wrangled a stretcher and chopper in high winds to pluck this needle from a haystack. And my utmost appreciation for the remarkable volunteers at Joshua Tree Search and Rescue, and the nurses and medical staff at the Desert Regional Medical Center.

Writing a book is quite a solitary journey, but so many people have been instrumental in bringing it to life. First and foremost, my super agent Sarah Williams. It's funny how life works and how people and places come into it seemingly at random – and yet, do they? You understood from the very get-go the story I wanted to tell, and I couldn't have done any of this without your patience, pragmatism and humour.

A most heartfelt thank you to Stephanie Jackson, Pauline Bache and the entire team at Octopus Publishing for getting behind my story with such enthusiasm and understanding, and turning my most difficult moments into something beautiful I can hold in my hands. It's a pleasure to work with you.

To my mother, Maggie: a big part of this has been your journey too. You came with me on the medical, logistical, physical and emotional rollercoaster, but boy, I'm glad we had that time together. Thank you for being there. And for the makeshift writing desk you and Tony set up under the window.

Caroline Nitsch, you have been my sturdiest rock even when the ground was far from solid. Acceptance and gratitude for all that you are. I couldn't do without you, mate.

My dad, Mike – thanks for your invaluable help while I found my feet in Vancouver, and for the regular messages of moral support. And Chris, appreciate you letting me bounce my rambling thoughts off you. (Sorry bro, I didn't get a chance to mention your 'towering intellect and stunning good looks' elsewhere in the book, so I'm dropping that in here.)

I'm grateful for the good folks of Joshua Tree who kept me in touch with the desert while writing, in particular Alison and Bryan Paris, Jef Harmatz and Jo Abbie (Jo, your sideline support and motivational socks made the creative process immeasurably better).

Big thanks to Melissa Roberts, for your friendship and support in Vancouver during the otherwise solitary months of writing. And a very special thank you to: Telli Nourkeyhani, Mara Ambrose, Emma Ventura, Signe Johansen, Henrietta Lovell, Fabiana Guglielmi, Richard Pang, Tessa Pritts, Sabrina Battaglin, Amelia Murray, Tom and Gayle Austin, Jean-Paul Garnier and Ash Crawford.

There are so many others not mentioned, simply because my gratitude could easily fill another book. But one more, for luck... Thank you, so very much, for reading.

ABOUT THE AUTHOR

Claire Nelson is a New Zealander who's spent more than a decade in London working in food and travel journalism. Her writing has appeared in titles including *Westjet, Delicious, ELLE, Lodestars Anthology* and *Jamie Oliver*. After recovering from her accident in California, she spent a year living in Vancouver, Canada, where she wrote this, her first book. Claire, her boots and her hiking stick are now back in London.

🐦 @clairenelson
📷 @ladyeclaire